Dearest Kitty

Letters from a World War II Sailor to His Girl Back Home

Kathryn Kimzey Judkins and Elbert David Judkins

DEAREST KITTY
LETTERS FROM A WORLD WAR II SAILOR
TO HIS GIRL BACK HOME

iUniverse books may be ordered through booksellers or by contacting:

iUniverse LLC
1663 Liberty Drive
Bloomington, IN 47403
www.iuniverse.com
1-800-Authors (1-800-288-4677)

ISBN: 978-1-4917-4164-1 (sc)
ISBN: 978-1-4917-4165-8 (e)

Printed in the United States of America.

iUniverse rev. date: 07/17/2014

Preface

The small envelope is yellow with age. The USO paper is fragile and torn. A six cent stamp with a picture of a propeller-powered bomber sits proudly on the upper right side of the envelope. There is no return address, just a San Francisco, California, postmark. But I know who mailed it to me, although I have not seen it for sixty-five years. I remember words from long ago, another time and another place. I was fifteen years old when he first wrote them. He was nineteen. The war went on and on for two long years. He lived on a destroyer, the *USS Stevens*, as a gunner's mate. He shot the big guns in many major battles.

We wrote often to each other. We waited for each other until the end of the war. I have more than one-hundred-seventy-six letters from my hero at sea. I almost destroyed them a long time ago. I thought they were too personal for others to see. But here they are. I want everyone to see this man I loved and traveled with for sixty-five years. It's good to remember.

Kathryn Kimzey Judkins
"Kitty"

Chapter 1

March31, 1943

An icy wind is blowing around the corners and down the deserted streets of Des Moines, Iowa. It carries an ominous message of despair that surrounds the small groups of people clustered around the boys who are waiting on the platform of the Rock Island train station.

The cry of a whistle echoes through the night. People move closer together, holding their sons, brothers, husbands and lovers tightly. How can they let them go? Many of the youngsters have never been away from home. They think they are men now. A terrible brutal war is being fought on far away shores and they are answering our country's call to serve. Our lad had enlisted in the Navy as the draft drew near. "At least I'll have a dry bed and three square meals a day in the Navy," he said.

Snowflakes begin to swirl about in the wind. I shiver and hold his cold hand tightly as the steam-driven troop train roars into the city. The large headlight on the front of the engine sweeps from side to side, illuminating the scene on the platform. It rumbles to a halt as military guards pour out of the warm depot yelling, "Say your goodbyes, boys. It's time to go."

Everyone tries to be brave. Our young loved one smiles and jokes and hugs those of us who are there to see him off. There are his brother, sister-in-law, my mother and myself.

I am only fifteen years old, he is almost nineteen. We have been acquainted most of our lives. I knew even then he would be mine forever but he still thinks of me as just a kid.

As he holds me tightly in his arms I feel him tremble. Is he cold because of the late winter snowstorm, or is it fear? He tries to hide them but tears glisten in his big brown eyes as he whispers, "Write often,

1

Kitty. Please don't forget me. Go on home now. There is no need to wait."

I can't speak because of the sorrow I feel. He turns away and marches bravely along with the others toward the waiting train.

Those in our group walk slowly to the old 1927 Model A Ford in the parking lot as the wind howls and the snowflakes fall. But I wait by the train. I can see him as he sits on the lower bunk in one of the cars. He quietly stares down at the floor with his elbows on his knees and his head in his hands.

I watch until my mother returns and says, "We have to leave him now. All will be well. You will be together again. Come along, we are about to have a big snow. We must get home soon."

April 1, 1943
Service Men's Center
St. Paul, Minnesota

Dear Kathryn,

Just a line to let you know where I am going. I am a little disappointed. I am in St. Paul now till 10:30 tonight. Am going to Farragut, Idaho. I am not supposed to tell this but I will.

It's snowing like heck up here today.

By the way, I never left Des Moines last night till eleven and never ate breakfast till 10:30 this morn.

They told us last night before we left that we were to march in pairs and were to let no civilians go between our lines even if we had to sock them. We knew last night where we were headed but of course this was after I saw you.

This USO is sure a swell place. A soldier said that you wouldn't find anyplace where they would treat you any better.

Gosh! I've got a lot of time to kill. Most of it will be spent in the USO. There's everything to do here.

I can't understand why we were sent north to get to Idaho.

I slept in an upper bunk last night. I expected to end up on the floor but I didn't.

Well, Kitty, this will be all for now. I will write you more later.

Don't write till you hear from me in Idaho. Love, Bert

How exciting to get a letter from a service man! Of course, I took it to school to show to my friends. How lucky I felt. He was most certainly the best looking boy in Warren County, maybe in all of Iowa. The girls were crazy about him but his first letter came to me.

Bert had been orphaned since his fourteenth birthday. He "batched" with two older brothers in their old farmhouse after the death of his parents. He was used to saying and doing pretty much as he pleased with little or no supervision. I hoped he wouldn't get into trouble doing things that were against military regulations, things like writing in his letter to me, "I'm not supposed to tell you this, but I will."

April 6, 1943
Farragut, Idaho

Dearest Kitty,

["Dearest"! He called me "Dearest"!]   *"Well, I finally arrived at Farragut. We got in here at 3 o'clock Saturday afternoon and had to get up at 6 o'clock Sunday morn. So you see we've got off with a good start. We get no liberties for four weeks because we are under quarantine.*

These boys who have been penned up for three months are going crazy to find someone they know from home.

This is sure one heck of a camp. There are mountains on every side. All the boys say we'll be sorry we ever enlisted and, boy, I believe them.

There are one-hundred and forty-five men in this company. They include cowboys, Mexicans, negros, Italians and about every other nationality.

Last night, our bags were searched for playing cards, dice, whiskey, etc. They told us what we had to send home. It included everything but our shaving kits.

We get our uniforms Monday. We also have to take another examination. I sure hope I don't make it.

They told us if we pasted a man here it meant sixty days in the brig. I won't send this letter till I get a return address but for gosh sakes answer at once because it takes about a week and a half for our mail to start coming. You know that's a long time.

3

I want you to give my address to George [Snodgrass, Bert's best friend from home and my cousin] *and the rest and tell them to write because I'm going to be very busy.*

This is Sunday and I thought I'd better write while I had time.

The next time anybody tells me the Navy will let us smoke anytime we care is crazy, because we can't even smoke on the grounds, although that won't hurt me. We do have good chow so far.

You know if I can't find better train connections than we had coming out here, I won't get to come home because we were on the road from Wednesday night till Saturday afternoon.

We also don't get but five dollars pay this month. I think we only get twenty-five dollars while we're in boot camp. Then when we get out they pay us in full to come home.

I'm out of smoking [cigarette tobacco; Bert usually rolled his own cigarettes during this period of his life] *and by gosh they won't let us go get any till further notice.*

Well, I guess I've rambled long enough, so tell everyone hello and tell them to WRITE!

Love,
Bert

PS. Didn't get to mail this yesterday. I had a very big day. Four vaccination shots. Also, I received all my clothes, $300 worth. Hurry up and write.

I had another letter from my sailor! I gave his address to everyone he knew and urged them to write to the homesick boy.

I was young and our world in south central Iowa was small. The only news about the war came from a twice weekly newspaper and from the radio. There were also news reports at the local movie theater on Saturday night, after the previews and before the cartoons.

In the beginning I didn't realize how serious the war situation was around the world. I was only concerned about when I would get another letter from my handsome boyfriend.

In those days everyone was fiercely patriotic. The Stars and Stripes flew from front porches and in windows all over town. We shared letters from our servicemen with our family and friends. Many more of our young people were drafted into the military and sent to faraway places. The dreaded telegram, "We regret to inform you," had arrived at a few homes in our area. Everyone grieved with the unfortunate families.

How exciting all of this was to me! How handsome the boys in uniform were!

I wrote to my sailor almost every night.

He endured another physical examination and passed it. I knew he would because he was a healthy, strong farm boy.

April 7, 1943
Farragut, Idaho

Dearest Kathryn,
Another day has just begun. I have just an hour before I go on guard so I'll drop you a line. I wrote two letters last night, one to Helen and one to George. I expect Indianola is very dead since I left.
I think I'll like the Navy fine if I can just get out of this camp. By the way, there's six camps right here together.
My buddy is that Cornell boy from New Virginia. He's a swell guy.
I feel right at home here because I've had overalls on since I've been here. I've never scrubbed the deck as yet but only because I don't stick my neck out for it.
Tell your mom that I'll have to take her advice because the Navy men don't drink or gamble. We had our baggage searched for dice and cards. I had two decks of playing cards taken from me.
For breakfast this morn we had beans and onions. It didn't agree very good with me but I had to eat something.
I haven't saluted an officer yet but only because I had my hat off in his presence.
Well, Kitty, I must quit and get the line in the mail. Write me, for goodness sakes. Tell your folks to write, too, and I'll answer.

Love, Elbert

I was not happy to hear he was writing letters to Helen, one of my many rivals for his affection. And I don't think my mother believed he had reformed. She hated drinking and gambling, a couple of vices our sailor enjoyed occasionally despite what he writes in this letter. Years before, she had nursed his mother when he was born. She thought that gave her the right to lecture him since his mother was gone.

Chapter 2

Growing up in small town Indianola, Iowa, is good. Everyone in the community is either a relative or a friend. It is strange when our young men are called into the military. Today they are with us, tomorrow they are gone off to some unknown corner of the world to fight a war most of us cannot understand.

Almost every week a military bus drives off Highway 69 and turns a corner at Salem Street that leads to the center of our town. A quaint old stone courthouse stands in the middle of the town square. Stores, cafes and beer joints surround the park like area around the courthouse. That's where some of our sons and loved ones board the bus.

Many days, as youngsters walk to school, joyful sounds of a marching band fill the air. Mr. Grange's high school band always sends the boys off to war with patriotic and current musical favorites ringing in their ears. High school girls rush to the scene and hefty farm boys and football players hoist them to the windows of the bus where the girls enthusiastically hug and kiss their heroes goodbye. Flag-waving citizens cheer and clap as the bus drives away.

Jobs in our area are scarce. Large ammunition factories are being built in various places around the country. For the first time in my life, people are moving out of our county. Women are going to work in the factories beside the men who are not in the armed forces.

Everyone in my home is excited. My two older brothers had moved to California a couple of years before. They write glowing reports of the many job opportunities and the large amount of money to be made in airplane factories and shipyards out there. My father and his brother own and operate a small Plymouth-Dodge automobile agency in Indianola. New cars are not being manufactured now because all of the metal is being used for the war effort. My parents have nothing to lose, so they decide to move to the land of opportunity, California.

I have not told my sailor of our grand adventure. He will not be pleased we are leaving the old hometown. He is having a difficult time adjusting to life in the Navy. He does not need anything else to worry about.

April 9, 1943
Farragut, Idaho

Dearest Kitty,

How are you making it back in good old Indianola? And it is good old Indianola. Gosh! I wish I were home with you. Every time I pull your picture out of my pocket it makes me wish this and I'm not just kidding.

I even stayed away from supper tonight to write you. About all the letters I have time to write is one a night. The reason is because we don't have any time in the morning or noon and we have to shave, take a bath and make our hammock in about 2 hours and one-half. I do have time tonight to play baseball. We play Company 220.

It's been raining today and has been rather cool. The weather out here agrees with me, though, because it's just right for the kind of workouts we have. Tomorrow night I have to wash all of my dirty clothes for inspection Saturday. Imagine me washing clothes.

I heard a lecture today from a very high officer. If I'm not a changed guy when I come home it won't be his fault.

We really have a swell company commander here but some of the fellows have been abusing some of their privileges so our liberties are liable to be taken from us.

I have guard duty again tonight. It's from four in the morning till six. I'm the guy who tells the fellows to hit the deck. I just guard the barracks here but it's a great responsibility. That too was what our lecture included. If you go to sleep on guard duty you can be placed before the firing squad.

I and ten other men from this company worked up in the hills yesterday, building commando trails. I have sores all over my hands. This wouldn't have happened but there's a lot of sickness in camp. Three more companies were quarantined today. The recreation hall has been closed, also the ship service.

Tell Richard [my younger brother] *I'll try and write him but I'm really busy.*

I got my Navy haircut today and, boy, was it short.

I sure wish my mail would hurry up and start. Tell everyone back there to write when they find time. As for you, take time. Do you understand? This is an order.

Well, honey, I must quit. With lots and lots of kisses,
Elbert

PS, I wish you could see me in these infernal boots!

There were so many changes for our young sailor. He has only been away from home for nine days but it seems like an eternity to him. Being homesick is one of the worst illnesses of all. I know he is suffering.

Our whole world is changing. Rumors are rampant about food rationing, gas rationing and other strange things for the civilians. Everything must go to the war effort. All of the school children collect scrap metal for the military. Old metal of every kind is gathered together. Front yards all over town have piles of metal waiting for big trucks to pick them up and take them to who-knew-where to be melted down. It is then made into guns and ammunition, tanks and ships and airplanes for our fighting men.

Daddy and Uncle Paul lock the door on their small automobile agency for the last time. Mother begins preparing for our big move to California.

> *Elbert D. Judkins*
> *Co. 223-43-3rd Reg.*
> *U.S.N.T.S.*
> *Farragut, Idaho*
> *April, 10, 1943*

Dearest Kitty,

How is everyone at home? Gosh! I'd love to be going to the show tonight with you. This will be another Saturday night spent wondering how things are going, and to think I even have to retire at 8:30.

You know, if things go well I'll be home in about eight weeks because I imagine I'll go to sea in about ten weeks. I hope so because I'll really be free then. A sailor aboard ship gets a leave or liberty every time the ship docks. Most of this company is going to sea so I'll probably stay with them.

We had inspection but I was lucky because I was standing guard at the hospital. I stood guard over there yesterday from 8 to 12 and again today from 8 to 12. Yesterday morning I was up on guard from 4 to 6 but when I get in 60 hours I'll get a stripe and I guess that's what I'm working for.

By the way, we lost one man from our company yesterday. He went crazy. He had a wife and two children that he left at home. There's really a lot of homesick fellows here. I get kinda blue once in a while but that's as far as it goes. It doesn't do any good to want to be home, as you don't get to go.

These officers around this company are swell fellows since we made a few changes. I even get to write this letter on government time.

You know I don't get but twenty-five dollars while I'm here and the rest when I leave so I'll really be able to have a swell time. Ten dollars of that comes at my first liberty. I aim to go to Spokane. That liberty comes in two more weeks and I'm really looking forward to it.

There was a slug of sailors left camp this morning, headed for home on leave.

I did my washing last night. Baby, I sure make a good woman. I haven't seen whether it came clean or not. A guy has to have everything just so here. I'm supposed to shave everyday whether I have a beard or not, but of course I don't.

My smallpox vaccination is really sore. I haven't had my other shots as yet. I hope I don't get them.

Last night my buddy went on guard at 12. He had to wake me and tell me I was lying on the floor, so, you see, my bed is rather a hard one. That's the first night I rolled out.

I finally got some candy last night at the ship's service. I had to go up after a Blue Jackets Manual. This is a book that tells the Navy way. It also gives 11 commands you do while on guard duty. You have to learn these or else.

I'm looking for some mail about Tuesday. I hope I get it.

> *Your loving boyfriend,*
> *Elbert*

I would love to be going to the show that night with my handsome boyfriend. Imagine him going to bed at 8:30 on Saturday night!

He thinks he will be coming home on leave in about eight weeks. I know I will not be here in eight weeks. Many other girls will be happy about that.

Mail must be the most important thing in a serviceman's life. He begs people to write him in every letter.

Two days later he is so depressed. He knows we are going to California to live. He knows I will not be here when he comes home.

> *April 13, 1943 Elbert D Judkins AS*
> *Co. 223-43-3rd. Reg*
> *U S N T S*
> *Farragut, Idaho*

Dearest Kitty,

I received your letter today and was never happier to get anything in all my life. I'm really down in the dumps. I don't seem to care whether I live from one day to another. I stuck my neck out one jump too far when I picked between the Army and Navy. I don't blame anyone for not wanting to go to the Army or Navy. It's really heck. Today we were up at five, ate chow and had drills, strength test, swimming test and had to go on a commando hike. I failed even the swimming because I was just too soft and short-winded to take it.

I was really disappointed to hear that you are going to California because I'm afraid that when I get my leave you won't be back there in Iowa. I sure hope so. Whatever you do, keep in touch with me and before I go to sea I do want to see you. I might be sent from the West Coast and I'll sure look you up if you are there.

I hope to be out of this hole in at least six weeks but I could be disappointed.

I don't understand why you had to get my address from Iris [Bert's sister-in-law]*? After all, I wrote to you first and I followed up with three letters, a letter every day.*

Whatever you do, if you don't hear from me, keep writing as we've had a case of scarlet fever in our camp and I might be next. Haven't you received any of my letters at all?

There are sure a lot of sick boys and men in here tonight. There were a few who passed out today on the strength test. I never passed out but I found out I wasn't a man as yet but I will be before I leave here if it takes them two years to make me. The older ones were the soft ones. Right after this came swimming and I was too tired to swim but 25 yards. All my liberties are liable to be taken from me, but I don't give a hoot. I don't care to go anywhere anyway. I finally had to swab my first deck this morn.

Well, Kitty, I must close as I want to get a little rest tonight. Tell everyone back there to write and I'll answer every letter I have time.

Love and kisses,
Elbert Judkins

P.S. Don't get the idea from this letter that I'm homesick because I'm not very. If you could only see the tears and knew the way I felt and I'm not kidding neither. I don't care if they do think I'm a sissy.

He is so young, and so very far from home. His new life is strange to the farm boy from the Midwest. The world is in turmoil and he is thrust into the middle of it whether he likes it or not. We are worried about his depression and are helpless to do anything about it.

I decide to write to my cousin, Neil Foust, who is in the Army. He is wise, and has always been a faithful friend to Elbert.

April 15, 1943
Fort Pike, Arkansas

Dear Kitty,

I don't know whether I owe you a letter or you owe me one, since we both probably got our letters about the same day, but nevertheless I'll write and get straightened out.

So Bert's going to Idaho. I understand that state is colder than ---- in the winter but since he'll only be there this summer (probably), he should hit some nice cool weather. I hope he finds things out in the Navy that will make him like it so he will get along OK. And don't worry about him saying he'd just as soon be killed as come back. He'll find out if he ever gets in a pinch, that he wants to live and come home just as bad as any of us. It was just the discouragement of having to leave home that got him down. He'll come around all right. If he'll only forget that damn stubbornness of his for a little while.

You said it had been warm back there in Iowa. It's been warm here too. Real warm through the days but the nights are perfect. We go back into khaki tomorrow and believe me, that is going to be a relief. These O.D.'s (wool) uniforms are really hot for as warm as the weather is. It's clouding over and looks like rain now.

I finally got off night duty. That is really grand. Seems good to be sleeping at nights now, and to get to go to a show again.

I thought for a while I was going to come home the middle of May but I know now that is impossible. Our outfit has cancelled all furloughs for six weeks so they can get caught up on their training program. This will make me come home in July some time. Be nice if I could get home for the 4th of July.

Well, I don't know much more to add now, so I'll close with

Lots of love,
Neil

April 15, 1943

Dearest Kitty,

I got your letter today and it sure cheered me up because I've really been blue. You know I didn't ever dream the Navy was like this. I thought it was a cinch but it's work!

You're busy from the time you get up till night and sometimes even after night. Everything's so much different. Today we went out for practice with rifles. I never was so tired when night came. [This from a farm boy who had worked like a man since he was ten years old!] *We went on a hike over the commando trail. It really makes one tough. The first thing you hit is a wall you climb with ropes, then another wall you climb over next was a tanglement, then you jump many ditches and last you march the rest of the time.*

Kitty, you asked me if I said that I didn't care if I never came back. Well, I guess that's true but not the way you took it.

You know there's a lot of men in the service with children, wives, etc. I figured they needed to come back much worse than I. Of course, there's <u>you</u>, but you're single and can always find someone else.

Kathryn, I at last saw a girl out here. Some officer's wife I suppose. I went up to have my identification picture taken and she was there.

I went to ships service last night to get some paper. They only let us go once a week. I guess all my liberties have been taken from me so you know I won't find any girl to go with. I honestly wouldn't anyway because I hope to see you again.

Well, honey, I've got two more letters to write so I must quit.

Love and kisses,
Bert

P.S. The other night I gave a quarter for a candy bar and tonight I gave a dime for an apple. Keep writing.

How sad to think that now his greatest pleasure in life is an apple, candy bar, and a letter.

Chapter 3

Our household in Indianola is in turmoil. Mom and Dad have found renters for our home and have reserved two rooms to store our furniture and personal items in. They will be here for us if we decide to return home from California.

Spring in Iowa is a lovely time of the year. The lilacs are beginning to bloom, as is our old Jonathan apple tree outside my bedroom window. Robins sing and collect string and things for their nests. Do I really want to leave this place and go to California to live?

The terrible war rumbles on all over the world. Young men leave for military training every day. My personal sailor continues to write letters to me almost every day. I will not be home to greet him when he returns from basic training on his first leave.

April 17, 1943

Dearly Beloved,
["Dearly Beloved"? That does not sound like my farm boy.]
I feel like the very devil. I had another shot and I can't even lift my arm. It really hurts. There has been a bunch of sick sailors here. Several had to be taken to the hospital. It just made them pass out.

I sure am glad to get your messages and I can imagine what Indianola is like. I wouldn't trade places with anyone back there. I'm learning to like it but I sure wouldn't want to go through with what I've gone through with.

I sure wish you weren't moving till after my leave but I am sure you will like it in California. I know I would. Listen, Sweet, if I get but a very short leave I'll be down to see you and I'm not kidding. Of course I'd like to see Iowa at least once more before I start to work on the Jap's, but I hope to get back.

I really have a swell buddy here but I guess we'll be parting because he is going to the Naval Air Corps. I've sure learned a lot out here but I was already a man before I came in here. [True, he has done the work of a man since his Papa died when he was ten years old.]

It was you that changed my ways and I'll always remember that resolution I made you. [What resolution? I wish I could remember.]

Is the war over yet? Gosh! I haven't even seen a newspaper since I came here. We're not allowed any papers whatsoever.

I've never had on my dress blue and I hope I don't have to put them on. All I've worn has been overalls and shirts. They really make me feel like a farm boy instead of a sailor.

We had inspection this morn but I was gone and was I glad cause there was a lot of heck popping. This morn I met an officer and I couldn't even raise my arm to salute so I had to bend my head to meet my arm.

[I think a gentleman officer should have said, "At ease sailor," and not expected him to salute under the circumstances.]

Well, Kitty, take care of yourself and keep those letters coming, if you will.

Lots and lots of love,
Bert

P.S. Tell Barbara Jean to send me her address.

I still have all your letters that you have sent me. I'm going to have them framed.

[He sends lots and lots of love now. I am beginning to wonder, does our innocent little fling mean more to him than I realized? He is almost twenty years old, and I am almost sixteen. Of course I love him as a friend, but is there more?]

April 18, 1943

Dearest Kitty,

I just wrote yesterday but I'll write again today. I spent another Saturday night in bed. Isn't that heck? I'm afraid I'll get to thinking this is home and want to remain in this camp. (Like heck.)

Today is Sunday, a day of leisure, I hope. You know life is getting softer every day. I'm beginning to get the hang of things. I know when to get in and when to stay out.

You know, I quit smoking for a week but I started again because I know where to slip to smoke. They say you can do anything in the Navy if you don't get caught. It's just got to where I don't care for nothing only of course I don't aim to get in serious trouble. Minor offenses aren't bad. They usually take your liberties from you and my first has already been revoked.

Guess what, last night I ran into Donald Sargent here. He's in Camp Peterson. He's leaving Tuesday for a trade school. We had a very good visit for about an hour. He gave me a lot of advice that he told me to take.

He told me to get in a trade school and he said that it was very possible that I'd be out of here in five weeks. I sure hope so.

Honest, I really like the Navy, but I hate this darn camp.

I sure was sorry to hear that Helen is engaged. I just about fainted. (Ha.) Listen, young lady, you really don't need to stay home or not go with the boys for me. Have a swell time, but take my advice, there's lots and lots of those boys not nice enough for you, and I'm not kidding. Do be careful who you go with. As for Earl, I think he's a pretty swell guy although I don't know him very well.

[How sweet, him giving me advice about other boys.]

I bet you can't name a thing I haven't done now. I sure have scrubbed my share of the decks.

This afternoon I have to wash, if the wash room isn't full. You know there isn't to be any dirty clothes in the Navy and I sure have my share. I hid them for inspection Saturday.

Well, Sweet, I must close as I can't think of anything else to say.

Love,
Elbert

It is almost time for mother, little brother Richard and me to leave our home on East Salem Street in Indianola, Iowa, and head for the far western shores of the U.S. I have mixed emotions about going. I love our old home that is next door to Bert's brother's home. I love our friends and family, but we all are so excited about going to Los Angeles,

California, and seeing our brothers and their families out there. Daddy cannot go with us as he has business to take care of in Iowa. He will be in California in a few months.

Folks warn us we will be closer to the awful wars on the West Coast. We are not afraid.

April 19, 1943

Dearly Beloved,

The weather today is cloudy and damp. Tomorrow is a big day with plenty to do. I'm kinda homesick for you, dearest Kitty.

I start the day at 3:30 in the morn. I'm on guard duty from four till six so I'll not get much sleep tonight. I sure hope it stops raining as I hate to be on guard in the rain because you absolutely can't leave your post. That's tough if you break any of the 11 orders you are given.

This place has really been a mad house the last few days. The boys have harps and an accordion here so we all gather around and think how well we'd like to be home. I'd give the world to see you. Listen, Kitty, whatever you do, if you have your picture taken send me one please. Every night I take my pocketbook out and look at your picture. It really looks like you could talk. I also look over all the letters you have sent me. They do help keep my mind off of home. Well, its 5:00 o'clock and at 8:30 I will have been up exactly 18 hours and don't think I'm not tired.

My pal went on guard the same time I did last night. While he was on guard the Battalion guard happened along. My buddy happened to have left his post for a short time to see another fellow. The Battalion caught him off his post and told him to repeat the 5th order. That order is, "To leave my post only when properly relieved." I don't think they will do anything to him but it will teach him a lesson he should never forget.

Well, Babe, I got seven letters today but not the one I always look for: The letter from you. I got one from Carolyn. Boy, I was sure surprised. I also got one from Leota. She told me all about George. He's a darn fool and I am going to tell him so.

[What did George do? I don't know. He probably partied a little too hardy. I think Bert wishes he could have been with him.]

I wrote to him the other eve before I knew Carolyn wanted me to do her a favor. I hope they do get together because they are both swell people. I'd never ask for a better pal than George and I'd really like to see him make something of himself and those kinds of parties will never get him anywhere, I know.

[George does make something of himself, big time, in later years.]

Our reports just came in for the boys to fall out that never passed their strength test today but at least I made it although I have some very sore muscles. There have been a few boys taken to the hospital because they overworked to pass it.

I expect this is kinda surprising that I wrote such a long letter but I'm really very happy tonight even though I am tired. I did find out something that I'm kinda sick of.

Today we heard a short lecture on trade school. I had thought I might try trade school since I saw Donald Sargent but if I am sent off to school I remain in the Navy for 2 more years. So, I know if I go that I'm in for at least four years and I can be transferred to the regular Navy for six years, which will make a total of 8 years. That would make me an old man when I got out and after all I only wanted in till the end of the war, but I stuck my neck out and I guess it's all for the best whatever that might be.

This morning going to chow the little German boy that marches right behind made a remark about drilling then he said that if us boys had been drilled like he had that we'd be alright. Someone asked him what that was. He said he'd been drilled never to fight against the German army. Boy, don't think that didn't burn me up because in the Navy you can't hit a person but if I catch that boy in any town around here me and him will tangle and maybe before if I can challenge him to box against me at the boxing club. I didn't ever aim to put them on because I do value my looks and I have enough marks on me from fighting already.

[My young sailor has always enjoyed a good fight, and he does have a few battle scars. They have not spoiled his good looks yet. He knows he is handsome.]

Just to show you the kind of Co. Commander we have I'll tell you what he did at Sat. inspection. We wouldn't have passed it and that would have meant 2 more weeks confined to the barracks but he beat the Capt. here and covered up for all the fellows. He put clean

towels where the dirty ones hung and so on. He's really a swell fellow even though he has given me ---- (censored) before. I can't think of anything else to say so will close.

Love,
Bert

We have almost finished our preparations for our move to sunny California. Gas and tires as well as many kinds of food, sugar, meat, shoes, clothing, etc. are being rationed. Government ration stamps are issued to each family. The larger the family, the more stamps are issued. Some people could obtain vouchers for enough gas to make a long move such as ours to California. However, many are riding the trains more than ever before. My mother and brother and I have made plans to take to the rails for our trip to the Golden State. We are almost ready to go.

Bert has only been in Idaho for 20 days, but it seems like a year for him, as well as for the loved ones at home.

Chapter 4

April 20, 1943

Dearest Kitty,

I don't have time to finish this tonight but maybe I can finish it tomorrow.

The Navy is getting better every day, but there are still a lot of bumps in it. By golly, it hasn't even quit raining yet.

I got a letter from you today. The only one I received but it was the main one. I signed the payroll yesterday but I don't know when I will get it. Money goes a long way here though, so it doesn't matter.

I took a GCI [Ground Control Intercept] *test today and I did my very best because that test follows me all through my naval career. If I pass it I shall go to school somewhere.*

I guess I'll try to get in naval aviation because I want to get out of this camp as soon as possible and there is no sea draft for ninety days and I would have to remain here as ships company, scrubbing decks and working in KP. By the way, I have scrubbed a few decks. I'll be a good hand at most anything.

A new bunch of recruits came in yesterday. There are some coming in about every day. So they are trying to get us out of here as soon as possible. I heard we have about four weeks left but we won't know till about a week before we leave.

I got a letter from Marsha West Monday. She also sent me some pictures of her and Homer. They sure were good.

What does Richard think because I haven't written him as yet? Tell him I'm busier than the very devil.

Tonight at 6 we went over to see a show on rifle shooting as we're going out to the rifle range to do some target practice. I don't like the way we shoot but if we rate high we get a 24 pass from camp. You know I want to get out and see what's outside of camp.

I still haven't had on my blue or white suits but I don't want them on. I want to keep them clean. I think the world of these clothes but I hate to wear anything but the overalls.

The lights don't go out tonight till 9 o'clock. A gold braid just came into the barracks. He sure caught a lot of fellows off guard. This is a pretty good company considering the kind of people we have here. Most of them are from California and Iowa. We go around and around arguing which is the best. Of course, you know the way I hang.

I sure hope your folks do change their mind about moving although I probably won't get home but I'm just afraid you won't like it out there. I'm sure I wouldn't.

Well, we just had a little excitement here. The fire whistle just blew and our barracks was supposed to be burning. Gosh, boys ran out of here barefooted and no clothes on and it was raining. I just had to laugh because I took time to even put my shoes on as I was undressed writing you because we can lay in bed with our clothes on.

April 21. Well sweet I just got back from the rifle range. I had quite an experience. Of course, they made us shoot the Navy way and that wasn't my way of shooting. I did very good though. I missed the bulls eye 4 times out of 30 but we only shot at a very close range. I really shouldn't have missed that because there were many that got a perfect score.

[Bert has the reputation of being a sharpshooter at home. He has been hunting and shooting a rifle with his older brothers since he was a young child.]

The sun was shining for a while this morn but it started raining again at noon. I'm sure tired of this ---- (censored) weather.

I have the afternoon to myself as some of the boys are not done shooting but I'm not supposed to write letters but you can do anything in the Navy if you don't get caught. Well, today I missed the mail call so I don't know whether I heard from home or not.

Sunday the 25th we are out of quarantine, then the liberties will start coming. We're supposed to get one Monday and then we can leave camp every other week till we get out of here. Gosh, there won't be anything to do as all the boys here will hit for the same town. I'll bet all the Sea Patrols will have to follow the boys from this company because the way they talk there will really be a bunch of drunk sailors. Here is one little boy that won't be because you can get into serious trouble over nothing and everything that happens will follow you through the rest of your life.

[Should I believe that? I don't think so.]

Have you been getting all of my mail? I've written you practically every day with a few exceptions.

You know they have an old tradition out here of having beans every Weds. and Sat. for breakfast, but it's getting so I don't mind them because after all my appetite is enormous now. I expect I've gained at least ten pounds since I've been here. I'm sure getting that old sailor tan and I expect I'm getting so I talk like these darn California boys. They sure have a funny way of talking. I just can't get along with those boys at all.

How is George performing lately? I wrote him and told him he was a darn fool. I sure wish him and Carolyn would get together but maybe if George doesn't want her and you move to California I might have a chance. Ha! What would you think of that? Helen Beck has never even answered the letter I wrote her but I guess I can understand why. You know there is really just one girl back there besides you that I like awfully well and that is Carolyn. I really think she's swell but of course I LOVE YOU THE VERY BEST.

[This is the first "I love you" I have gotten from Bert.

[I'm not worried about Carolyn stealing my boyfriend. She has been a long time loyal friend to me.]

I received my white clothes back from the tailor today. They were too long for me. None of our clothes are sent to laundry or they are never pressed but the Navy has a way of rolling clothes to put creases in them. We roll our clothes into rolls and then put them in a sea bag. Whenever we leave here we take our bed clothing and everything else. I put on my blues to see how I like them. About the only thing I like is the silk neckerchief.

If you ever want to see what I have gone through go to the library and get a Blue Jackets Manual. Everything in it is what is happening out here. The Navy is really nothing like they claim it is at the recruiting station. They only fill the boys there to get them to enlist. There are always certain times to do anything and there are all kinds of rules you must obey.

I really feel sorry for these married men with families at home because they are really homesick. There have been several boys in our company discharged. Some were injured while on the commando trail. They were hurt internally. I went out there the other day but I slipped back because I didn't feel like going on. Gee, I wish you were out here to enjoy the swimming. I'm quite glad that I didn't pass because I get to go swimming about twice a week. The next time I go up I'm going to qualify or else drown. I'm sure not turning around because I want a liberty.

[Bert said later he paid another sailor to take his swimming test for him, and he got away with it!]

Has Earl ever walked home with you again? You'd better get on the good side of George because he tells me everything that happens back there. He's really a swell guy. I'd sure love to be back there enjoying those parties he's having. I'm getting tired of this sissy life. You know I am built up now so I can take anything. I won't care how big a person comes anymore.

How's Stumps coming? Do you ever slip in there? I hope not because that's not the kind of place for you. I sure wish I'd hear from George more often. I know darn well he has more time to write than I. I wish he and Albert would come out here but who knows, the next time I move I may be on the east coast. I hope not, I still want to go to Calif. I have a very good chance no matter what I pick. Life here seems to drag so darn slow that I'm getting so I don't give a darn what happens. Here a person sees nothing, hears nothing and knows nothing. Well, Baby, I must quit as I want to write the girls. My sisters, understand?

Lots and Lots and Lots of Love and Kisses,
Bert

P.S. Not bad for me is it?

It is not bad at all for a shy guy. It is much easier for him to express himself in letters than it was in person.

The news of the war from around the world continues to worsen. It appears it will be a long, terrible fight before we have peace once more.

April 22, 1943

Dearest Kitty,

I finally heard from you after two days wondering. I suppose I can forgive you as I reckon you were busy.

I am awfully sorry to hear that Bobby has to leave this summer as it is awful for a man with a family to leave home. I know because there are a lot of married men in this company and they are really sick.

I really can't say that I like it but I will in time. There is an old man here that sleeps right across from me. He kinda helps cheer me up.

I wrote you one letter this evening but I tore it up because it sounded as if I were too blue. I really don't want anybody to get that idea because honest I only want out of this camp. I hate it here. Everything you do while in boot camp is work. Week from next week we go on KP and then that will be something for me to crab at because we get up at 3:30 and stop at 7:30 for one week.

Next week will be drilling for practically every day so I really want some letters to cheer me up. I think they are trying to rush us through here because there are a lot of new recruits coming in daily.

I will probably be one of those boys that will be put back about 75 companies. It has been done and I have a boil on my chin and if it gets any worse I will be sent to the hospital and if I'm kept there 3 days it means I start dropping back so something serious is going to have to happen to me before I go there.

I have been reading the Indianola paper but I haven't seen any news to speak of.

Listen, Kitty, I want you to have a swell time back home even if you do go with the boys. There really isn't much use of anyone planning on seeing me for about six months anyway and I'm not kidding. Of course, understand I don't want you to forget me. I really think a lot of you and I know you do me.

I promise deep in my heart I'll never do anything that I'll be sorry of, although at times I really don't care what happens. That is generally when I catch heck from some of my superiors and it really does burn me to take orders. Today I kinda hurt myself. I talked back to an officer but he was only a petty officer. That is the same as a sergeant in the army. We had been doing the manual of arms and I was tired so I stalled so I could rest and he seen me. He thought I didn't know it so I had to perform in front of the company and show him. I'm famous in this company. All the boys know me because I expect I get more heck than anyone else.

I really try but there are a lot of things I'm very slow in, especially marching. I take a stride longer than anyone else. I get out of step, and of course I get heck for this but it's getting so I can really take it. I don't care how much they yell because after all I aim to get out of this place, then things will be easier I hope. I want to get into the Naval Air Corps and see if I can't use my brain instead of the undeveloped muscles. I am going to try and take up something I can use when I get back in civilian life because it looks very much like I'll be in here for some time.

Tomorrow is field day. That is clean up day for inspection on Sat. I hope we get to sleep till 5:30 but I'm afraid we won't because our company all seems to be trying to take this thing not serious enough. I really get very tired myself but one person can't sleep in this bunch.

I wonder what will happen in Indianola Sat. night. I saw in the paper where Johnny McKee had a car accident. It really was too bad he didn't break his neck. I reckon that is an awful thing to say but I have no use for that guy. [Editor's note: Some years later, John McKee would marry Kitty's cousin, Marilyn Hess. John was physically abusive, however, and the marriage ended in divorce.]

I received a letter from a buddy in Miss. He's really homesick. He has really gone to the dogs so I won't mention any names. He did give me some very good advice. He's been in quite a lot of trouble over getting his leaves because he generally winds up trying to drink the town dry. He's been caught twice by the M.P. and he has had to stand guard 12 hours with a 60 pound pack on his back. So you see what can happen if a person doesn't have any will power. That is the least thing I think of. I don't even care for a liberty only to get to wander around camp.

I want to go over to Camp Ward to see a boy I got acquainted with coming out here. He was really a swell guy but nothing like the other buddies at home. I've heard many of the boys say that they thought more of the fellows here than the boys at home but I couldn't find a better pal anyplace than George. He's the swellest friend a person could have.

I expect to be separated from these boys as most of them are talking up something different. The Cornell boy is trying for the Air Corps also. We will know next week whether we make it or not.

I hope Toby wasn't hurt very bad as I know how well you folks like him. He surely tried to bite someone and they probably kicked him.

Tell the other girls and boys back there hello and tell that darn George to write me or he doesn't need to expect to hear from me again. Is George going with Carolyn yet? I hope so. I really like those 2 kids.

We have a boy here that's been in the Navy 4 years. He's really a swell guy. They offered him a rating today but he wouldn't take it. He said he knew what it was to have other fellows barking out orders. They asked him why he wasn't at sea and he told them his term had expired and then the Army caught up with him.

Today our officer gave us a lecture on gambling and drinking. He said that the Navy was like the Army that even though it was prohibited that it went on the same but not so much. If you are caught the punishment is very severe. There absolutely isn't any going on in our Co. though.

Well, Miss, it's about time for bed so I must stop all of this rattling and get some sleep. I'm on the deck scrubbing in the morning so I'll try to get a good night's sleep. Love, Elbert

Bert knows our move to California is near. Why doesn't he mention it? Does he think if he ignores it, it will not happen?

Co. 223-43-3rd Reg

April 24, 1943

Dearest Kitty,

I have time to write a few lines so here goes. I got your letter today, also one from your mother. Was sure glad to hear from you folks. The Navy is agreeing with me better everyday although I still have a lot of work to do. I could be busy all the time but I have to write a few letters. I really should wash tonight but there is always another day. I really have a lot of letters to write as I try to answer every one I get.

Yesterday I heard from Neil. He sure poured it to me and really gave me a lot of fatherly advice. He just told me to a T what I was going through here so I suppose the Army training is about the same as the Navy. We don't get in town as often as the Army but I'll bet you are glad of that. Ha!

Today we went to the boat races. They were really something to see and the lake, boy, I never saw anything so pretty. This afternoon we watched the boys parade. It was sure something to see and the band was really grand. It sure thrilled me to think that I will be showing off by the same band. The girls were really thick in camp today. Nurses and Waves were running everywhere. They also kinda caught my eye. Ha.

Say, me and this fountain pen are not getting along so good. So you will have to excuse my writing.

By the way, I guess my chances with Helen are gone forever. She wrote and told me she was engaged but another jealous girl had already told me. I really am glad you are jealous because if you weren't I would know you didn't care for me and after all you are the whole world to me. I hope you don't think this letter is mushy because really I am serious.

[We are both jealous of each other. It keeps us on our toes.]

The company in the same barracks as us have scarlet fever and are under quarantine so we may be next and to think that tomorrow night at 12 o'clock we are out of detention. This all just happened today.

It won't be long until school will be over for you so what are you aiming to do? Have your folks decided to move yet? Has George stopped his wild parties? Don't mind the questions because I only want to know what is happening back home. I have been reading the Indianola paper but there doesn't seem to be any news in it. I suppose you will be having or probably have already had a lot of fun tonight because it is 8 here so it would be 10 back there. Just think when you are up of a morning I am still lying in bed. This morning I was up at 4:30 because of inspection on Sat.

Kitty, tell your mom I will try and answer her letter next week as I have twelve letters to write and I have to study the Blue Jackets Manuel tomorrow.

I had another vaccination yesterday for something or other. It seems like my arm just gets limber and then they poke that needle into us again. They really don't care how much it hurts either.

My buddy is sure homesick. Tonight he is lying on his bunk not doing anything. Usually he at least writes home or is talking to me but tonight he is saying nothing. I haven't thought much about home as yet although I do think of everyone back there but really I hope to make something of the time I am spending here and I do have something to look forward to although some of the letters I get don't cheer me much. I got a letter from my brother and he said the 1st two years were the worst. I hope like the very devil I am not here for more than 2 years but I know I will be here that long and very likely 4 years if I go to school.

How did Toby get? I hope he is ok but I reckon he is alright.

Did Carolyn ever get my letter? I don't suppose she would tell you if she did. I would really like to hear more often from the folks back there. This mail is really funny. At first my mail came in 3 days now it takes four. It only took four days for Neil's letter to get here.

I can't understand why I have never heard from Kendall but I suppose he is too busy to answer my letter. Does his girlfriend ever step out on him? I sure hope she doesn't because Kendall told me if she ever did he was really going to start raising the devil and he wasn't kidding either. In the Army you can always find plenty to drink.

That's one good thing I will say for the Navy. We absolutely don't drink here and I'm proud to say that.

I just heard that we have a case of measles in our Co. so this means 1 more week of quarantine. Gosh! I hate that because we were to get a liberty Wed. and I wanted to go to Spokane but that's gone now. I'll bet a dollar something happens and I'm set back about 40 companies. The boys have just been pouring in here. Now there are 49 companies behind us and all of these have come in the last 3 weeks.

I have to scrub the decks in the morning, isn't that the berries when I thought I could sleep awhile anyway. I miss the sleep worse than anything else. I suppose you get plenty of sleep.

Does Barbara Jean go with any boys now? She told me she was through with them until she was fifteen years old.

Gosh! Kitty, I wish you hadn't told me about being down to Theo's for supper. It really made me hungry. I really have nothing like that to eat here. I have eggs but they taste like rotten ones. These are liable to come 3 times a day. We have fish on Friday. Most everything we have serves the purpose of hash! It's all just thrown together. We do have pie and cake once in awhile.

You know, Kitty, you said you wished I would get to leave this camp soon. Well I do too even if it would mean overseas service. I aim to get out of here even if I sign for sea duty. I do want to get into naval aviation so bad I can taste it.

By the way, me and my buddy were talking today. If anything would happen to me right now I don't have a darn bit of identification at all. Of course, he would know me. You know everything happens here. Today a boy passed out while standing at attention. We stood there for about 20 minutes.

Listen, Kitty, I sure love to get your letters so write everyday that you have time, please.

Iris and Theo are surely busy because I have only heard from them once since I have been here. I guess people don't realize how bad these boys need this mail. Really, if they went through with this they would because you are out drilling all day, you are dead tired and discouraged, honest, your temper even slips a little when you hear that mail call and you are really glad but after you stand in line for about an hour and no word from home you are back in the dumps again. So you see why I want letters.

The other day I was on the grinder. I was standing at the parade rest when I turned my head toward the C.P.O. He told me to straighten up but of course I told him that the Blue Jacket

Manual said you could glance toward anybody that was speaking to you. That night in the barracks I proved it. He's just a little man, no rating any better than a sergeant. Nobody here likes him. We had one before that was broken down and now we really pour it to him. I would sure hate to be that person. Well, so much for this, will write more later.

Love,
Elbert J.

Letters from home are about the most important thing in the world to a young military person. Their new life is so strange to them and they are homesick, bewildered and exhausted. How disappointing it is to eagerly await a letter but none arrives.

Our household is almost all packed up and we are ready to leave the old homestead. I don't think Elbert really believes we are going.

The war news from around the world is grim. More things are being rationed every day. New ammunition plants are opening all over the country, providing jobs for folks who have never recovered from the Great Depression years. More young men are joining the military and leaving home, many never to return.

Life in our quiet little corner of the world will never be the same again.

April 26, 1943

Dearest Kitty,

As how you say you haven't heard from me maybe I had better write. Sweet, I haven't by no means forgotten I have a girlfriend in Indianola. I really think of you a lot. I guess you are my dream girl. Last night I dreamed I was home with you, then I awoke. I about cried and I'm not kidding. I was never so disappointed in all my life.

So far I have heard from you pretty regular. If it weren't for you writing, a lot of days I would never get a letter. Listen, Kitty, I don't think I have missed writing you over twice. It really takes so long for mail to get anywhere nowadays.

Boy, life here is becoming easier every day. We still have about the same kind of work but my body is better developed and I can take it. Today we clumb [climbed] *ropes to build arm muscles. When we got in the air about 20 feet we had to tie a chair in the rope and sit in it. I had already learned to do this so I knew how. They say this has saved many lives.*

We marched by the band part of the day and went through the manual of arms. We drill quite a little yet but we haven't been out on the commando trail.

One of my best pals here has the measles so I expect he will be sent back several companies.

Next Sun. we are out of quarantine. We should have been this Sun. but those darn measles. I have signed for a liberty. I want to go to Spokane, Washington, but I have to be back by midnight and there won't be anything to do. I haven't gone up to get my dress jumper yet.

I wish you could see my picture on my identification card. I didn't hardly have any hair. I get one more Navy haircut then I can let it grow. Honest I can't even part it. It wants to lay every way.

Thanks a million for telling Albert to write me. Did I tell you that even if Helen is engaged she still writes me? She gave me a good understanding, though, that she is engaged.

I read the Indianola paper tonight also the Des Moines Tribune. We weren't to have these but they are here anyway. They sure didn't do much to those 3 kids from New Virginia.

Gosh! The Waves are sure getting thick here. They take the place of a lot of boys. A sailor absolutely can't date them though. I sure hate that! Ha! No, honest, all I think about is just leaving here and moving to a new destination. I'm too busy to go with any girls and besides I still have a girl in Indianola.

Tomorrow night is wash day. I don't have a very big washing but it is big enough. I wish you were here to help me. You could at least press them for me. In other words, I just wish I could see you.

I still have never had on my blue or white uniforms although I am really proud of them.

I saw my name in the county paper but I was looking for yours. I hope by this time you are feeling O.K. Miss, you said you were writing in bed. That is usually the only space vacant. Well, honey, this letter isn't very long, just a note to let you know I still love you.

Love,
Elbert

P.S. Mushy aren't I?

He is saying the three little words, "I love you," more often now. I am thrilled.

Chapter 5

The above is the last letter that I have from Bert until the last Of May. I wrote to him in May and I am sure he continues to write to me, but with our move out of the State of Iowa to the West Coast, many letters may have been lost.

Mother and Richard get on the train in Des Moines and head west one blustery evening in the first part of May. I have decided not to go on the train with them. My cousins, residents of California, had driven in a car from there to visit relatives in Indianola. They invited me to ride home with them. They are going to visit friends in Army bases along the way, as well as stopping to see their brother and family at an Air Force Base in Arizona. I think that is more interesting than a boring train ride.

We leave Daddy and Toby in a small apartment above the cigar store in Indianola, and our journey begins. Daddy promises to join us soon. I don't ask what was to become of Toby. I don't want to know.

After an exciting trip across mountains and desert we arrive in Los Angeles. I, a small town Midwestern girl who had never been out of the state of Iowa, am speechless with delight when we come over the mountains and see the bright lights of Los Angeles sparkling in the distance. Shortly after our arrival the "blackouts" in the towns and cities along the coast become effective. City lights are turned off as well as lights in the homes. Heavy curtains are pulled over the windows at dusk so bright lights will not attract enemy planes and ships that can be lurking out of sight in the darkness, just waiting to bomb us. We are settled in a rented home with my brother Tom and we wait for our father to arrive. Except for a little homesickness, we are happy living in the big city.

Dearest Kitty,

Gosh! Was I glad to hear from you. I really didn't look for a letter until next week.

You surely like California. Well, I'm glad if that is what you want. If the sun shines there it is nothing like Idaho. It either rains here or it is very foggy.

It is wash night for me so I probably won't get this letter finished tonight.

I want you to tell about your trip and then what it is like in L.A. I'm hoping I am either sent to Diego or the Great Lakes.

I'm supposed to get a fifteen day leave to go home but nothing is certain here. I probably won't get it.

I suppose I told you I didn't make the Naval Air Corps. They found something wrong. I guess it will be gunners mate. I hope so because it is likely I will be sent to Chicago. I could get home on liberty then.

Thanks a whole lot for the present, Kitty. I can sure use it.

By the way, be sure and send me your phone number. Maybe I can give you a call before I leave here. I don't suppose that will be very long now. Anytime after next week.

I've sure been getting lots of mail from the boys and girls at home. They sure hated to see you leave Indianola.

Tuesday we get another liberty. I'm staying right here this time. I lost too much sleep the last trip I took.

We really had a big week this week. I, of course, had to stand dog watch for one day. Don't think that don't get on a person's nerves. I was in a boiler room. The sweat just poured off me.

Next week we have to learn how to abandon ship, go through the gas chamber, go out on the rifle range and over the commando course, then we get to take off our boots.

I went swimming all morning. I really enjoy a good swim but all I know I'm afraid it won't do me any good at sea.

We just got out of quarantine last Monday. They sent a boy from our company to the hospital yesterday. He may have scarlet fever. It's really terrible here. The outgoing unit is even quarantined. All companies that graduate have to stay at the barracks.

You know, honestly, I hate it here. All the boys do. They treat us like kids. We get the very devil for everything. After all, I enlisted to get away from home and I guess I can suffer. Two boys awhile back tried to go over the hill but were caught. That would be a job here because these are really hills.

I'll bet you can't guess what happened. I got a picture of Helen Beck. Oh Boy! The worst of it is all the letters I write her are censored by Jim.

There are sure a lot of new companies here now. The boys just flock in. There are several boys here I know but I can't go to see them. They won't give me a pass to get by the guards. And you sure don't want to try and slip by.

I had cat fever a day or so last week. Don't think I wasn't scared. I figured right then that I would be here for the duration.

[Cat fever? What is cat fever? (Editor's note: This may have been a reference to acute catarrhal fever, a vague affliction often associated with sailors, frequently with symptoms similar to those of colds or various flu strains.)]

The way Barbara Jean writes George has sure changed a lot. You know I don't blame him a lot. There aren't many boys left at home. I expect if I were there with him that I would help him out of ditch. I don't know, though, it is really going to be tough controlling myself. I can sure understand why a sailor is wild when he goes ashore.

Well, Kitty, I must slip a cigarette and then retire for the night. I want to see if I can get a good night's sleep. We had to get up at 4:30 for inspection and then didn't pass it, so goodnight and

Lots of love
Elbert

He cannot wait to get out of the camp in Farragut. He is hopeful he will be getting a leave to return home. Most of his mates have gone on, why hasn't he?

Wed. May 26, 1943

Dearest Kitty,

I received your letter today. Was sure glad to hear from you. So you like California. Gee! It must be a pretty good place to beat Iowa. Sure wish I were there. Any place would beat this hole.

I've really been sick today. It wouldn't surprise me if I were getting scarlet fever but I won't go to sick bay till I'm packed out. We will graduate most any day now and I want to be in this company when that day comes.

We've had two days of liberty, one yesterday and one today. I stayed right here. I never even went to chow all day.

One good thing though is we haven't had to do anything. I'm afraid I'd pass out if I even have to stand at attention.

You think you would like to cross the ocean. I wouldn't mind being across but I don't suppose there is any bottom to that ocean.

I'm sure getting tired of just writing letters. I'd like to see you. Maybe I'll get sent to California. They have a receiving ship there. I've been hoping that the sea draft catches me. That is my only sure chance of leaving here.

I ought to be kicked. I haven't written a letter home for a week. Someone will be wondering what the matter is. I expect it will be another week before they hear from me.

I tried to get a pass to Camp Ward to see the boys over there but nothing doing. I was disgusted. You can't do anything here.

The boys are sure coming in here fast. Poor fellows. The Navy is swell but, gee, those first 3 weeks and then these hot days that are coming. It has really warmed up. The sweat sure does run while we are drilling.

Do you hear from the kids at home? They sure hated to see you leave. I got a letter from Neil today. Oh! Boy! Me and him went around and around. He thinks the Army is the <u>only</u> thing but not me. I told him it was very funny why a person in the Navy could be transferred to the Army. The Navy is first among all branches. I suppose the Marines are the toughest next to the Navy Hospital Corps.

Well, this isn't much of a letter but keep them flying until I write again. One more letter and I'll be moving, I hope.

Love, Bert J.

He hates that camp so. I hope he can be moving soon as well.

My family and I love L.A. Richard and I have learned our way around the city. We are thrilled to be living here.

May 29, 1943

Dearest "Kitty,"

I expect you have been wondering why you haven't heard from me. Well here's why I've been very busy the last day or so.

I was sick the first of the week. I at least got out of all the marching. I sure don't want to go through with those days again. The boys kept asking why I didn't go to sick bay but I wouldn't give in. They said they were going to build a pine box for me but I fooled them they didn't have to.

Say, the way you write it must be rather warm down there. I wish I could get a tan like you.

By the way, I learned what a sailor's best friend is. It happens to be a gas mask. I went through a gas chamber today. I stood in there about 2 minutes with the mask on. Then the order came to take it off. I didn't suppose there was any gas in there but I found out different. There was. It was tear gas. I sure did my share of crying because I was the last man out. I didn't think I could find my way out.

Kitty this will be the last letter you will get for awhile so you can stop writing until you hear from me. I'm leaving Tuesday morning for Iowa. We graduate at 6 and leave at 8:45. I don't know for sure but I think our company was in the sea draft. All the boys get leaves. So far no company but ours has all gotten leaves, just boys going to sea. They won't tell us till we get back where we are going or what we will do.

I have my leave papers and my ticket so I am hoping for the very best. I'd sure love to come down but I expect you will understand. Maybe I'll get stationed down there and then I'll get to see you. I sure hope so.

I don't understand why you haven't heard from me. I wrote two letters the first of the week.

I sure have a lot of work to do before I leave. I have to wash my clothes and my sea bag before Monday. We have bag inspection Mon.

I got two letters from my sisters. They're sure worried. I haven't written them for 2 weeks. I don't blame them much. I expect they will be a little surprised to see me because they don't know I'm coming. In fact, I didn't know for sure and I'm not gone yet.

I'm going to send you my watch one of these days for a keepsake. It's not much but the Army and Navy have both had it.

[I think his brother, Homer, the Air Force man, gave it to Bert.]

This isn't much of a letter but I have to write another one to an aunt in Texas. Homer and I can't keep in contact for some reason and she's worried. He isn't getting my mail and he doesn't know my address so I'm signing off until later.

Lots and Lots of Love
And Kisses,
Bert

I wish he could come to Los Angeles on his leave, but I understand why he would want to go home to Iowa. He has a big family and a lot of friends in Iowa, and only me in L.A.

Chapter 6

Bad news travels fast. Bert has not been in Iowa on leave long before letters from relatives and friends begin to arrive telling of his bad behavior in the old hometown.

Who can blame him? A handsome young sailor who has had his life changed and disrupted and he now finally has a few days of freedom. He has been homesick and depressed and disillusioned. He's home again and having fun. But I think he feels a little guilty about it now.

June 17, 1943

Dearest Kitty,

I'm really ashamed to even write you but here goes. I expect you have heard by now what happened in Iowa. I wouldn't blame you a darn bit if you never wrote me again.

I haven't heard from nobody since I got back to Idaho. My back mail has never even caught up with me yet.

How is California by now? I sure hope you like it. I'm sure it's a pretty good place to live.

It's really pouring outside tonight. It's been raining here for the last three days.

Say, I'm really blue tonight. I was supposed to leave tomorrow for an unknown place. I was going to gunners mate school. What happens? We go in quarantine for seven days for something. I'd sooner bet nothing.

I'm sure getting tired of this Out Going Unit. All we do here is lay around and smoke. We could go anywhere but now we stay right in this barracks.

Our old company was split up into various camps. There happens to be four boys in here with me. We get to go on liberties the same time. *They divide us up into liberty groups. Each group goes on liberty every third day. I have more liberties than I have money. I'm supposed to get paid Sat. but I suppose that will be cancelled.*

Tell Richard I saw Toby when home. He's sure a lonesome boy. He's not satisfied anywhere.

These darn boys are driving me nuts. They never go to bed until 11 and oh! the noise they make. We get up here at 8 and retire at 10 and sleep all day. I get so much sleep. I lay awake half the night. I don't know of anymore to say so I shall sign off.

Love,
Elbert

Write me here.

Elbert D Judkins S/C
Co. 223-43-O.G.U.
Barracks-8
U.S.N.T.S. Farragut, Idaho

Poor little Toby dog. That bit of information does not cheer me up. I'm beginning to be a little homesick.

Elbert D. Judkins S2/C
Co. 223-43-O.G.U.
Barracks-8
June 22, 1943

Dearest Kathryn,
I'm really sorry I haven't written more often because I'm not doing a thing. The way you sound you are a trifle homesick. Gee! I wish I were in California. Maybe I could cheer you up. I know how you miss the friends at home but truly there isn't anything to do in Indianola and you'll be O.K. as soon as you know someone. I don't suppose I'll ever be satisfied for anything now. I'm not the same guy you used to know. I'm just a little wilder than I used to be or else I just don't care what happens next.

I watch every draft that comes up and where my buddies are going but still I hang here laying around. It wasn't bad at first but I'm ready to go to work.

I received 20 letters today. It was all back mail but one from Homer. He said he'd reached his final destination.

Say, what did you mean when you said I'd forgot you? Really I haven't but I just don't like to write letters anymore.

I think I told you I got my school. It's a 16 week course on guns. Then I'm going to try and get on a merchant ship. I don't suppose I'll make it.

My buddy leaves Friday. I don't know but I think he'll stay right here for 3 months. I sure hope I don't. I was supposed to leave last week but I am still here, but the next draft I'm leaving or else.

Monday night four boys in our barracks were caught gambling. All the money laying on the table was taken from them and they had to go before the Captain. It so happens that I was in bed (broke).

Well, this isn't much but there isn't anything happening around here at the present. Do write.

Love, Bert

Elbert D. Judkins S2/C
Co. 223-43-O.G.U.
Barracks-8

June 23, 1943

Dearest Kitty,

I hope everything is alright with you. How is California life by now? I sure would give the world if I were only there. I'd give a lot if they would only ship me out of here.

All I do is smoke, smoke and smoke. I'm really getting tired of waiting but I guess all I can do is wait.

What is Richard doing? Does he like his new home? I'll bet you can have a lot of fun there. The way you sound there is surely a lot to keep a person amused. I'd like to see what it was to really enjoy myself again. Things aren't the same anymore. I guess the world is changing more and more.

Well, the sun is shining for another day. It is still rather cool here but I don't suppose it gets any warmer. The snow has left the mountain peaks though.

My last buddy leaves tomorrow for an unknown place. Gosh! I guess I'm going to be the last one after all. I sure wish I were going with him.

He is just a kid, 17 years old, and he was selected for sea duty. He never realized what he was getting into till tonight but now he is rather blue. I can't help but wish he were here and I were taking his place. I will at least be here for 16 weeks.

I'm supposed to get a 48 hour liberty tomorrow but we had another case of scarlet fever break out today and we weren't supposed to get out of quarantine till tomorrow morning so I won't get to go. All drafts leave now regardless so I'm thankful for that.

I got two county papers today but I guess I can't even tell any news from home. It is really hard for me to write anymore. Nothing happens here, I guess.

The other day I was down at the ships service and I did run on to a boy I knew. He was on mess detail and has been here for 7 months. Poor guy.

Well, Hon, I haven't forgotten you so please write.

Love and Kisses
Bert
S.W.A.K is on the back of the envelope.

Our sailor is depressed and discouraged. It seems he is stuck in Farragut while all of his friends are being sent elsewhere.

We in California can see giant searchlights scanning the skies at night, searching for enemy planes. We hear large guns on the coast being shot out over the water and are told the Coast Guard is just practicing in case we are attacked by the enemy.

Meat and other commodities are becoming scarce. Mother is proud at dinner one night because she had bought some meat at the store. It smells good while she cooks it and it is delicious. Later we found out it was horsemeat, and was not rationed. It spoiled my taste for meat for a long time.

Elbert D. Judkins S2/C
Co.223-43- O.G.U.
Barracks-8
June 26, 1943

Dearest Kitty,

    Well, how is the girl and California coming? I hope you like it fine by this time. I also hope you are not quite so homesick. You can't fool me. I can tell by the way you wrote you were pretty darn sick. I guess all I can do is feel for you because I'm not there to cheer you any.

    A lot of new drafts came in a bit ago. Here's hoping I'm on one of them even if I go right to sea. If I miss one more that is where I will go. That would be one sure way of getting out of here.

    I was sent out for work today again. I worked too. Gee! But it would be grand to get back in school. At least I could use what little brain I have. I guess I'm really getting lazy. I don't care for nothing anymore.

    It has been raining here all day today. I guess that is about all it knows how to do. The weather is really very disagreeable.

    All my buddies have left now. I'm with complete strangers again. I don't know who I can trust and who I can't.

    I hear from George once in awhile. He's working for Conklin's yet. He's really a swell guy. I guess Kendall is seeing it pretty tough. I can't understand why he never picked the Navy with me. He was going to once. I don't care to lay around but darn those packs, I wouldn't care to carry one of those around. I don't know but I don't think his girl is true blue to him. I don't blame her a darn bit but I hope he never finds out if she isn't.

    I did get out of quarantine yesterday. And I'm not back in yet. If I'm still here Sunday I am going to try again to see the boys I know. "If at first you don't succeed try, try again."

    Tomorrow is Saturday, a day I hate to see come. Everything has to be too clean. In fact, spotless. Some guy got my sheet dirty tonight so I'll have to cover it up some way.

    How far are you from San Diego Naval Camp? I think I'll be sent there or back to the Great Lakes. Very likely to Diego. That is where my pal went. He was a great pal too. Before he left he gave me a silver dollar for a luck piece, one he had carried for a long time. His name was Edwin Prothero. He lived in Des Moines. He was a handsome boy, seventeen years old. I was with him on the way home. He told me he got engaged while he was back.

The poor guy didn't know what he was in till he was selected for sea duty.

I'd have given the world to have changed places with him but there wasn't any way I could.

There are sure a lot of boys coming and going every day.

Most of the boys are kids. They don't realize how serious things are till they go.

I wonder where Neil is now. Is he still in L.A. or do you know? I haven't heard from him for some time. To tell the truth I haven't heard from you for a long while. I don't know whether I don't get the mail or you don't write. Anyway write with,

> *Love and Kisses*
> *Bert*

How sad, his friends have moved on, and he hasn't.

> *Elbert D. Judkins S2/C*
> *Co. 223-43-O.G.U.*
> *Barracks-8*
>
> *June 27, 1943*

Dearest Kitty,

Listen, please don't think I've forgotten you. Honest, I've written you a good many letters. They surely aren't reaching you. This letter of yours was written and mailed on the 21st. Today is the 27th. So you see, the mail is very slow and uncertain.

I'm sure sorry you have changed your mind about California. I'm certain you will like it better when you get acquainted and most of all over your homesickness. You are homesick, aren't you?

Do you think you will go back to Iowa? If that is what you want I sure hope you can. I prefer Iowa myself but I guess I've got a long wait coming before I see it.

So you know your way around somewhat. Well, it is rather fun to ride streetcars.

Well, I was called out for work today at the receiving unit. They asked me if I could type any, so I had a pretty good job although I never had very much typing.

Gee! But I'd like to see you. I'll bet sunny California has really put a sun tan on you. Myself, I am a pale little boy. I'm inside the majority of the time.

All my pals have left me here alone. Boy I sure wish I had been selected for sea.

I guess I picked a pretty tough branch. There was a big write up in the paper tonight about gunners mates. They said if we wanted some action to get in this. I'm afraid it will take a person with more nerve than I have but one thing for sure, I'll try it. You have to weigh at least 150 lbs so I'll have to eat like heck because the last time I was weighed I only weighed 145. The first was 131, so you see the Navy feeds us although it isn't so good at times. I won't touch fish anymore because they run that stuff in the ground.

Today has sure been a swell day. The sun was shining so pretty and to think I couldn't even get out in it.

All these boys are blowing tonight is how drunk they got while they were on leave. They just came back and every darn one is from California and Washington. I wouldn't brag about it if I were them. It isn't anything to be proud about. Take a tip from me, don't ever fall for the Navy boys. Every one is the same. I've seen boys here that never took a drink before get drunk. In fact, going home I helped take care of a boy in my company. He was headed for Chicago. He was picked up in St. Paul by the S.P. and was taken on home. He was put on report and after his leave was thrown in the brig. He was a darn swell kid while he was in boots, too. I can understand why it is though.

Another week has slipped by and I'm still in O.G.U. I can't understand why they don't call me. Sitting here isn't helping any. I just as well be stationed on a farm. At least I could be busy.

Well, to get back to letter writing. I heard a boy say he lived in Des Moines so I had to inquire a little.

There is a boy here playing the guitar and singing. If he doesn't keep quiet he will have me crying and I'm not kidding either. He can sure play but I just want to be let alone. I don't feel like friendship tonight.

So the kids back home don't write. Well, I promise to write every day I have time, so that will likely be every day because I have more time than I know what to do with.

Well, I didn't get your letter done last night so I shall proceed to finish it. The sun is really shining so I had to hang up a washing. I washed my dress blues and I'm keeping my fingers crossed because they might shrink a little.

I am going to try and get in Camp Ward today. I don't suppose I will succeed but there is nothing like trying.

There is sure a mess of boys leaving tomorrow. Included is an E.D. Judkins but it isn't me because the serial number isn't mine. I'd like to run on to him and see what he looks like.

I smoke a pipe now. I got tired furnishing cigarettes for all the boys. Don't you think I'd look ducky with a pipe in my mouth?

I ran into an old school boy the other day. He's in ships company here. He said he was going home for a fifteen day leave just to Seattle. Some guys I guess are lucky. This makes his second leave while he has been here.

I also ran into a boy from St. Mary's this morning at the mess hall. He is getting a Medical Discharge. He sure hates to leave but I suppose it is for the best.

Sickness has broken out here now so next week I expect I will be shipping out but there is nothing certain. I suppose all I can do is wait.

Well, Kitty, I must write some more letters so I had better sign off.

Lots of Love
Bert

Elbert D. Judkins S2/C
Co. 223-43-O.G.U.
Barracks-8
June 28, 1943

My Dearest Kitty,

While I sit here with a Coca-Cola in my hand I shall drop you a line. I'd give a lot to see you if it were only for a short time. I guess it will likely be a long time though.

Tomorrow I'll know my verdict. I'm supposed to leave if I can pass another physical examination. I don't know where I will go. Very likely I will stay in Farragut and go to school for four months. I hope not.

I sure hope I get a letter from you today. I haven't heard from hardly anyone for several days. I think my mail is getting lost.

Say, George has sure changed. He works very hard but he is plenty wild. I don't blame him. He is only young once and if he ever gets in the service you grow old fast.

I'm by no means an old man but I have to take things too serious. A person can't do anything but what he is breaking a rule. I can take any order from anyone but some things are carried plenty far.

The weather is sure swell up here now. It is so nice and cool but the sun shines so pretty. If only there was grass to stare at in place of rocks.

Well, back to letter writing. I just finished cleaning up and making my bed. It isn't very late but I'm in need of sleep. After Taps there is as much noise in here as before.

Gee! I hate to think of wearing blues all the time but when school begins I'll have to.

Kitty, by all means keep writing because I'm positive I will stay in Farragut. I don't mind too bad because I expect there are places much worse. Maybe I can get the 4th off. If so I think I will go to Seattle to see if I can locate my aunt. I wouldn't know what to look for as I never ever seen her.

I did a very silly thing yesterday. I washed my blues and of course they shrunk up. They fit plenty snug now.

Well, I found another buddy here. He is going to gunners mate school with me but something will happen. One of us will be scratched.

They discharge a good many every day with various things. Many have nervous breakdowns and I can sure understand why. I've about went nuts laying around myself.

I expect by this time surely some of your Iowa friends have written you. I sure hope so. Maybe you will get over being homesick. I can feel for you because I'm a trifle homesick myself.

Well, Sweet, this isn't much of a letter but I have another one to write so I had better close until later.

All my love,
Bert

Yes, I am a little homesick for my lifelong Iowa friends, but it is nothing compared with the sickness our young service people feel. They are standing on the brink of the unknown, terrible wars are raging around the world, and soon they may find themselves right in the midst of the fighting.

Elbert D. Judkins S2/C
Co. 223-43-G.M. School
Barrachs-8 Lower
Camp Peterson
June 30, 1943

Dearest Kathryn,

Gee! Am I disgusted. I guess everything goes wrong with me. It so happens I got my school but I stay in Farragut. I wanted this least of anything. It's too late now or this boy would go to sea. Why unload my troubles upon my girlfriend?

By now I suppose the weather is really hot down there but I bet you really have fun or is there such a thing anymore?

It looks like I spend the 4th here. Boy, that is heck. Life starts anew once more. We get up at 5, go to bed at 9. School is from 8 to 11 and 1 till 4, six days a week. I don't mind that but we drill and exercise, so you see I'll be busy the majority of the time. Please don't expect too many letters. I'll write every time I have a spare minute. I guess I'll try to locate my mail this afternoon. I know there are some letters someplace.

I got one letter this week from Homer. He told me he was seeing plenty of action but not to tell the girls. I sure wish I were with him instead of in this place. Actually this is a dirty place. No grass, nothing but plain rocks.

This letter is not very interesting so I shall close.

Lots and Lots of Love
Elbert

Elbert D. Judkins S2/C   **U.S.N.T.S.**
Co.223-43-G.M.School   **Farragut, Idaho**
Barracks-8-Lower
Camp Peterson

When my sailor is unhappy, he calls me Kathryn, not Kitty. And he closes the letter, Elbert, instead of Bert.

What can I say? His disappointment, hatred of the camp, homesickness and worry all speak clearly in his letters. His words tell it all.

But he handles it well, and conducts himself as a young military man should.

His brother Homer is in the Air Force, and is in the midst of combat in the Pacific war.

Chapter 7

Elbert D. Judkins S2/C
Co. 223-43-G.M. School
Barracks-8-L
Camp Peterson
U.S.N.T.S.
Farragut, Idaho
July 1, 1943

Dearest Kitty,

How is the old girl making it? I hope everything with you is swell. Every time I sit down to write you I really get the blues. I guess I get to thinking of the swell times I spent with you at home. No kidding, I've got a real lump right in my neck now. I guess the good days are gone but here's hoping they return again and soon. Gee, Kit, I know I've really not been true blue to you but no fooling, you are the most wonderful person I've ever met and wherever I go I will always think of you and I sure hope you don't forget me. I'm going to see you once more if it is the last thing I do.

I've got a good many things on my mind now. I can't help but worry about Homer but I feel sure he can take care of himself. I got a swell letter from him the other day. In it was forty dollars so I guess he still thinks I'm a kid unable to handle my share of the business. I guess I must be capable or I wouldn't be going to school.

[Bert is the baby of a family of ten children. He is special to all of them.]

I started to school this morning. I didn't think at first I would start till next Monday but plans were changed.

I'm in something I can't get out of now, so they tell me. I guess there are two ways to get out, to graduate or be packed out dead. I chose the first. I'm sure of another rating and if everything goes O.K. I will become a 3rd class Petty Officer. If I am, I can stay here as an instructor or be transferred to a ship. I'm taking the last because I have a duty to perform and I plan on carrying out my part.

[I'm proud of my young man.]

Life changes for me every day. I will be busy the majority of the time. Please don't expect too many letters from me but always remember I love you with all my heart and I will think of you even though I am busy, so write whenever you can.

I'll bet your little brother is homesick, isn't he? Tell him I said hi. I suppose you of course hear from your dad. Is he coming to California or do you plan on going back this fall? I plan on getting another leave in November but I am afraid I'll be needed at sea too badly. Until later

Your loving boyfriend
Bert
XXXOOO

Elbert D. Judkins S2/C
Co. 223-43-G.M. School
Barracks 8-L
Camp Peterson
U.S.N.T.S.
Farragut, Idaho
July 3, 1943

My Dearest Kitty,

Nothing to do so here goes with a note. Maybe by this time you are not quite so peeved at me. Are You? Now be truthful. It really doesn't matter even if you didn't care for me, I still couldn't forget you. Boy those sisters of mine sure raked me for the way I behaved on leave. They were afraid I would be AWOL coming back.

Gee! All the boys in this barracks are on K.P. but little me. I guess I'm lucky in one sense but I will lose some sleep tonight as I'm on guard watch.

Tomorrow is the 4th of July and am I sick. No liberty but we can run over the camp. I'm not going through boot camp over, it might even be worse. They really keep us jumping, also they are building us up more and more. I suppose it is all for our own good but I really don't care for this type of training. If I knew all I do now I would be sailing the sea. I could work up the same way and there would be a chance for a miss step. Here I can fail easily and still not mean to. If there were only some way to back out. I guess I have no confidence in myself. I was always taught this meant sure failure.

Kit, I'm darn anxious to hear from you. It's been a mighty long time since I received any mail. I know there must be a pile of letters somewhere.

I'm really a tired body this afternoon. The chief came in and rolled us out early for some uncalled reason. You know they punish a person funny here. If one person is to be punished the whole group is. I don't exactly believe in this.

Smoking is prohibited inside the barracks. We smoke after breakfast and anytime we have time. (Before breakfast if you don't get caught.)

Well, I didn't get this letter finished yesterday so I shall carry on with it. Imagine what, I didn't get up till 7:30 this morn. Nobody called me so I slept. I was on guard last night so I didn't get any more sleep than usual. I really had a time trying to do my duty. In fact I couldn't carry it out so I let it ride because I didn't care to club anybody, although I was plenty mad at times.

How's Richard and your mother? I suppose they are silly about California. I wouldn't care if I were there myself. I think it would be a swell place to be.

Gosh! But it is really chilly outside this morning. It doesn't look like I would have any trouble sleeping of a night because of the heat. It does warm up during the day but so far it has been swell for July.

Gee! Where was I last fourth? I can't recall but I believe I was out with your cousin. I expect we were painting all the towns red. I hear he was home for a furlough. I'd have liked to seen him. We have some hot times over the Army and Navy. Of course you know which is by far the best. To be honest, I don't. I know the Navy is tough and I don't know what the Army is like.

It won't be long till a certain person has a birthday will it? Sweet seventeen [It is sixteen. He is wrong.] *and never been kissed. Or has some boy kissed you in California?* [No.] *The way these California boys talk, they have no good lookin' girls there, but I know one there now. Watch your step. I hear there are several sailors in L.A.*

Carolyn Killam won't answer any letters anymore. She really told me off. [I don't think I want to know what he did while home on leave!]

When I was in O.G.U., I really had life compared to here. I believe life at sea couldn't possibly be any worse. Honestly, Sunday is the only day I have spare time. You know I will have to start studying now, or will I? I haven't decided whether to work hard and try to become a 3rd class G.M. or not to work as hard and become a 1st class seaman. I believe the last would be best. At least I wouldn't have so many responsibilities. I don't feel capable of a 3rd class G.M.

Well sweet, I must get this letter in the box.

All my Love and Kisses
Bert

Elbert D. Judkins S2/C
Co.223-43-G.M.School
Barracks 8-L
Camp Peterson
U.S.N.T.S.
Farragut, Idaho

July 5, 1943

Dearest Kitty,

I have time for one short letter so I'm sending it to you. I really don't have time either but just the same I'll take time.

Gee! But I've really been jumping. I haven't had a spare minute. If we don't have to study we have to box. I drew a pretty good size man and don't think I wasn't pushed around. The only thing I watched was my face. I don't care to be cut up. I already pack one scar caused by my entering the Navy. It has been a long time since I've been so tired and sleepy.

The day has been very hot here. The first hot day we have had here. By the way, what did you do the 4th? I didn't do anything. I did have all the ice cream I could eat but that wasn't what I wanted.

If nothing happens I will get out of school in October. I hope it doesn't happen because I don't care to be here this winter. It would be terrible. We have personal inspection every morning before classes. You really have to dress here. I washed my blues again tonight. I don't care to take any chances.

I guess this is just a line but I must get my clothes and hit the bed.

Five is plenty early for me. Well, Sweet, I promise faithfully to write more next time.

All my Love and Kisses
E.J.

The 4th of July is a big holiday back home. With the terrible war raging, it will be even better than ever this year. Everyone is patriotic these days.

Elbert D. Judkins S/2C
Co. 223-43-G.M.School
Barracks 8-L
Camp Peterson U.S.N.T.S.
U.S N.T.S.
Farragut, Idaho
July 7, 1943

My Dearest Kitty,

I finally heard from you. I got a letter today mailed the 30th. The addresses on it made it look like it had been around the world. My mail is everywhere on the station but none of it seems to find me.

So you are a soda jerk. Well that isn't a bad job. I wouldn't mind having a soda right now. It is so beastly hot here today. I sure hope it doesn't stay that way.

And you still don't like California. Maybe when your Dad arrives there you will like it better, do you reckon? If you want to stay there for me you had better stop waiting. I expect the war will be over before I see the sea. I hope so. I wish they would make San

Diego my home port though. If ever I come there I'll see you if it is the last thing I do. I look to be sent there around the last of November.

So Evelyn took you out for dinner. [Evelyn Akins is my brother Tom's sometimes girlfriend. Whatta gal!] ***Don't write that way. It really makes me hungry. The last few days they have tried starving us here.***

You say nothing ever happens there. Well, there is too much going on here. It may look like school days because I do carry a book and paper but it is a long way from school. Here if you skip class or lose a book or even have a dirty hat, it means Captains mass. There is no monkey business here in school. After school we have boxing and wrestling and everyone takes part.

What is Bobby doing now? I'll bet his baby is sure cute but if you stay around long I expect it will really be spoiled. Ha!

Tonight as I write this letter I think of what fun I could be having with you. Gee I'd give the world just to spend a day with you on the beach. I have my shirt off right now. I've been boxing outside and I just took a shower. Every night I lay outside till Taps, sunning my back. I've begun to get a tan now.

Saturday and Sunday is liberty. All I plan on doing is picking up my pass to get out of work. I like a few hours to myself. Really I should be studying now but I'm not and I don't plan to. If I can't get a rating without working all the time I don't want it. I'd like to go to advance school if I can and a rating won't allow me to.

Gee! But I pity the boys in boot camp. It would really be hot out in the sun all day. There are a good many boys here from Indiana, but to see them is impossible, I guess. I do see Lavare Cornell about every Sunday. We generally go to Area J ship service and eat ice cream all day. It isn't so bad here but there must be places that are better. The thing I hate worse in school is that we can't sleep in class. I can't get enough sleep at nights here.

Kitty, if you don't hear from me very often, please don't think that I've forgotten you. I'm very busy and I have very little time to write.

I met a boy here in this company from Iowa. I met him once before when I was working in the northern part. He's a darn swell kid but I don't know but what I made a big mistake the other day. I loaned him $15.00 to send back home to a bank. At one time he *was in a car wreck and got in some kind of trouble. I may never get it back now and my pay number is mixed up some way because the 5th I went to get paid and they had scratched me off the list.*

Well, sweetheart, I must get this mailed so I shall close.

All My Love
Bert

Elbert D. Judkins S/2C
Co. 223-43-G. M. School
Barracks 8-L
Camp Peterson
Farragut, Idaho
July 9, 1943

My Dearest Kathryn,

Since I don't have anything to do in class I shall start a letter your way. I just took a test a few minutes ago and I'm anxious to see if I failed. My brain don't function as it did a few years back but I'm pretty sure I made it.

I got another letter from you yesterday that was written the 1st of July while I was still in the O.G.U.

I'm beginning to like it here better every day although I hate to get up in the morn and take those darn exercises. I'm so sore I can hardly move.

Kendall surely is seeing it tough. I really can feel for him because I've had a taste of that stuff myself. Those drill days are over for me now. My work is brain from now on and am I glad. Of course I'm specializing in guns and someday I'll be behind a big gun. It will sure be tough on him if he doesn't get to go home on a furlough but I think surely he will before he goes across. I don't expect I will get home again but there is always a chance. I really don't mind. I'm anxious to get to sea myself. I'm a sailor and I've never seen the ocean.

Kitty, the way things look now I may be sent to California to advance school, if I'm not too dumb, of course. I hope they send me out on a merchant boat. I'd like to get on as small a ship as I can because the officers in charge aren't as tough.

When I was home, Kendall's girlfriend wasn't stepping out on him. I really believe she's O.K. although one never knows. One thing for sure, if she ever does Kendall won't be the same guy I know. Do you suppose Kendall will get to see you? I know it will be a long, long time before I do.

Today is the last day of school for me this week. I was supposed to get a liberty but instead I'm on watch or guard. This is the berries, too. It happens to the best, I guess.

So you have a lot of company huh? Well that is something. I'd like to step in for a short visit myself. Noise is something I'd like to hear instead of someone shouting knock it off. We don't make noise in school and I'm not kidding.

Well, Kitty, this letter is stating nothing so I shall stop.

Love,
Bert

P.S. Hope you like your job O.K., and listen, Miss, what do you mean by saying "I hope I'm still your girlfriend"? You know darn well you are.

UNITED STATES NAVAL TRAINING STATION
Farragut, Idaho

July, 10, 1943

Hi Honey,

I will probably have a time writing this as I am laying out on a mountain peak, writing this in the sun.

Today is inspection day so had to ship out of the barracks. I really enjoy this anyway. It is about the prettiest place I could locate.

There is a big group of boots a little way off and I have been talking to them. They are in Camp Hill.

So you even take care of the place by yourself. Say, Miss, watch those sailors. You might find one you like. I'd be lost clear out then. It's tough not being able to see you but I guess nothing can be helped.

[The manager of the drug store where my little brother and I work must trust me, an ignorant little country girl, and my brother. He often leaves us alone in the store. We cook breakfast for the customers, and I shudder to think about those meals. I am not an experienced cook.

[As for finding another sailor to take my man's place, it will not happen. I am in love with BJ.]

Gosh! But I could just about go to sleep but I'm afraid a snake might curl up in my pocket. I can't spell yet or even write so please excuse me.

Gosh! There are sure a lot of boys running the Commando course. I have to run it twice a week but it is really good on a person. I may be a man someday. Who knows?

What's this about calling you a little girl? I guess I can if I wish or can I?

Say, you do write to me fair. Maybe you think I am going to forget you. Listen, honey, I really think the world of you. I know I've broke some promises but it is darn hard not to. Please don't think that I've forgotten you even if you don't hear from me. I'm generally busy. Today is liberty day but I'm staying here just to write and do up my work. It looks like rain anyway. There really isn't much to do in town and I need the rest.

Well, sweetheart, this is short but I want to get back to mail call. I'll try and write a long one tomorrow.

All my Love
Bert.

The war news from around the world is grim. Rationing worsens, food and gas and tires are almost impossible to get. The big guns on the shore boom at night, as searchlights cross the California skies. And our young men die on foreign shores day by day. Uncle Sam in his red, white and blue clothing and striped hat points from posters everywhere, "Uncle Sam Wants You!" In just two more years, I shall join the Waves and sail the seas on a hospital ship. That is my dream. What a wonderful day that will be.

Chapter 8

Elbert D. Judkins S2/C
G.M. School Barracks 8-L
Camp Peterson U.S.N.T.S.
Farragut, Idaho
July 11, 1943

Hi Good-looking,

I can't think of much to say but I'll write a few short lines. I guess I don't like to write any better than you.

What are you doing? Still a soda jerk? Gee, would you give me a soda if I dropped in to see you?

If you should wonder why I write in pencil it is because I'm out of ink. I'd rather write with pencil anyway.

I just got back from Camp Ward. I went over to see the boys from Indianola but they have all gone home on leave. The lucky devils are supposed to get 21 days. Some guys are lucky but they will find out that the real life was while they were in boots. I did.

Did you ever eat horse meat? [Yes!]

You know, I could be mistaken but I think that is what I had for supper last night. I do know we eat a lot of goats and sheep that is about as bad.

Gee! Today is a swell day to lay in the barracks. I wish you were here for a few days. You could really enjoy yourself if it were only for a visit, but to live here would be terrible.

I went over to the drill hall last eve and played a game of basketball. We have a lot of recreation in Service School.

So you think you will go to school this fall in California. I was talking to a boy from Des Moines that was inducted the same day I was. He's going to Treasure Island. He is in the Armed Guard. I wanted in this but was too light. I guess I'm just a kid although I don't like for people to tell me so.

Gosh! I know several people here now. I get acquainted with more and more every day. It is really a pretty swell place after all.

Yesterday I was up to see Lavare Cornell. He has been up before Mast for not changing his mattress cover. Boy, inspections in the Navy are strict.

Do you work awful hard, Kitty? Gee, but I'd love to see you. If things go the way I hope I'll be out of here in about 11 more weeks. If not, it will be 15. Then I want to be sent to California. Here I will try to get put with the Merchant Marines.

I got a letter from George the other day. He's really working. He said as soon as he is 17 he is going to enlist in the Navy. I think everybody believes it is a cinch. I expect they have the same opinion I did but they will learn much different or maybe they like the Navy uniform better than some others. They do attract girls, ha!

I really am proud to be in the Navy myself but it is no place for a good time. Whenever you see a drunk sailor, don't ever get the idea they all are that way. There are a good many that are but we learn cleanest and we really must be clean. Take the Army. I don't believe in running one down because we are both fighting for the same reason but the Army can drink on camp and they also can play cards and shoot dice. We can't.

Yesterday I washed a pair of blue pants. This morning they were gone. Some guy I suppose needed them, now I have to make them up. Thank heavens they only cost $4.50.

Well, honey, I rung on long enough so I must stop. I got a letter from my aunt today. She asked if I had a girlfriend in Iowa and told me to tell her all about her so send me your life history, ha!

Love and Kisses
Elbert

Elbert D. Judkins S2/C
G.M. School Barracks 8-L
Camp Peterson U.S.N.T.S.
Farragut, Idaho
July 12, 1943

My Dearest Kitty,

I guess I can't get my mind on school work, so I might as well write you a line. I'm in class right now taking notes on my school work. Gee! But I think of you a lot. I guess that is why I can't study. It is about time for school to be out for another day. One very good thing is time flies. It really doesn't seem that I have been gone almost 4 months.

Kitty, I want to see you so bad but, gee, don't be disappointed if I don't get to see you. Really, I believe by the first of November I'll be on the ocean somewhere. I really don't mind this part so bad but I would like to see everyone again.

I saw in the paper where Neil Foust was called back to his base before his furlough had expired. Is he still here or do you know? I sure hope he isn't across. I never thought much about it till I see my closest buddies leaving.

Gosh! I have about a mile to walk and it happens to be pouring down rain.

I finally got here and I'm really wet. The little water won't hurt me because at noon the dust was terrible while marching to school. I sure wish I were out of this place but I'm not.

I expect I am in trouble today. We have roll call three times a day. It so happened I didn't attend the muster so I'm on report. I slipped off and went to chow. I'll probably just get some extra duty. Here's hoping I don't have a check in my records A.O.L.

So you would like to go back to Iowa. I don't blame you a darn bit but I myself will never be satisfied at home. There is something about the Navy that you dislike and still you don't care to be out. Even your Mom is homesick. That's surprising but I guess everyone can get that way. There were two young boys in O.G.U., about 16 I imagine, that cried every night when they got into bed. I felt sorry for them but they were not the type that wanted pitied.

By the way, what is your little niece's name. I can't remember whether you told me or not. [Mary Jo]. *I had an idea that it looked like you. It would be cute then.*

So you hope someday we can have fun like we use to. So do I. If only we get back to Iowa once more together. We will have the time of our life. Yes, I remember how you used to hate Indianola. I felt the same way but it would look O.K. only if I went back I would rather see a certain little girl by name of Kathryn Kimzey waiting there for me. Only I wouldn't blame you for not waiting.

Listen, sweetheart (if I may call you that yet), you need not write me everyday although really you don't realize how glad I am to hear from you.

I'm sure glad you like the place you work. It really gives you some way to pass the day.

I received a letter from a pal of mine that went through boot camp with me. He was drafted to the shipyards in Washington.

Well, honey, I can't think of any more to say so I shall close because I have an awful lot of work to do before bed time.

Love and Kisses
Elbert

Elbert D. Judkins S2/C
G.M. School Barracks 8-L
U.S.N.T.S.
Farragut, Idaho
July 13, 1943

Dearest Kitty,

I don't have much time for writing but will write a line. I should really be studying but it is very hard to concentrate on my work. We have tests at the end of every week but all I can do is hope like heck I make it.

Are you working very hard these days? I'll bet it is fun to mix malts. If you could eat all you wanted, I'd like that job although I'm afraid I would eat away the profits and lose a job.

It will soon be two weeks of schooling for me, only 14 more to go. Golly, but that seems like a long time to be marching to and from classes. I would lot rather be second class seaman instead of a sailor at land. It is very funny, some get a rating by hard work, others just get one. I guess I will get mine by the hard knocks.

Do you hear from Carolyn? She doesn't write me anymore. I guess she hasn't forgotten the way I acted at home. I get several letters from different kids around Indianola but I haven't heard from anyone the last three days.

Golly, I wish you could see what we have for a mascot. It is the sweetest little pup. The boys brought it back from liberty last week. It gets the very best to eat and is really taken care of.

I sure have been rushing around here tonight. I washed and cleaned up and now I'm going to finish this letter and then study. I have guard duty 2 hours Thursday night and also sea bag inspection so I won't have time to study for my test that we have Friday. These tests are the way they decide who gets a rating.

I saw in the Indianola paper where Donald Mills is an Ensign. Gee, I'd sure hate to have to salute him but I'm glad to see him get his rating. Heaven only knows he earned it. Every rating is earned, don't worry.

The silly guard in the barracks last night let us all about freeze out. The windows were all open and instead of him closing them he put on his overcoat to keep warm himself.

Well, Kitty, I haven't been tattooed yet. I'm about the only one that hasn't. Some of the boys have them all over. I think the first time I'm in town I'll get my service numbers and name put on me. It is one sure way of never losing it.

Well, sweetheart, I must close for now. Write me whenever you aren't too busy.

All my Love and Kisses,
Elbert

His letters sound so young and innocent. Do these lads really know what lies ahead of them? Bert wants his identification numbers tattooed on his body, so he won't be lost forever if the unspeakable happens to him. All he really wants is mail. He begs for letters every time he writes to me.

Elbert D. Judkins S2/C
G.M. School Barracks 8-L
Camp Peterson
U.S.N.T.S.
Farragut, Idaho
July 16, 1943

Dearest Kitty,

I've got a million letters to write but here goes with the most important one. I got your letter yesterday. I can't understand why you get two letters in a day from me sometimes. Several times I've gotten two letters from you but I understand why. They send my mail to Barracks seven and then I finally get them.

So you have a girlfriend down there you would like me to meet. The way you write she must really be swell. I wouldn't mind meeting her. As for me, I would rather see you. Do you realize it has been a whole four months, about, since I've seen you? That is a long time when I had seen you about every day.

I'm glad you like California better and also your work. I hear a lot about California. If it's as good as these boys say it must be perfect. We have a good many boys here that went through boot camp at San Diego. They really hate it here. I guess myself I really can't say I hate it because it is the only camp I've seen. Some day this will be the largest and most beautiful naval base in the United States.

Well, Kitty, I'd like to tell you about my work but I can't. We aren't supposed to talk to anyone about nothing. All I can say is it pertains to the operation of guns. I really wish I had nothing to do with it now. It is by far a harder subject than I ever thought. I really don't expect to get a rating from it because there are too many boys smarter than I.

Last night we had another sea bag inspection. This morning we had a test. You really don't have any time to do any studying so you see why I don't get grades. The reason is because I write letters when I should study.

Did you by any chance know Gene Woods from Indianola? He went up for induction in the Navy and didn't pass so he's going to Seattle. He's coming by Farragut so I wrote and told him to stop and see if he could get in here. Indianola ought to be full of sailors now. There were at least 5 boys went home last week from here. I wouldn't mind if I were with them but at least I can keep out of trouble here.

So you think you might move. Where would you go or would you still stay in Los Angeles? Well, it is about time for lunch and physical fitness. Today we have a real rough game. They call it push ball. All it is to see how many can come back inside without any scratches. It's too tough to suit me.

I've lost track of several buddies. I wonder where they can be. Is Neil still in Louisiana? I haven't heard from him since I was in boots.

Tomorrow is Saturday, the last day of school for another week. I guess we have inspection by the Commandant and a Rear Admiral, so I'm going to be busy washing clothes etc. tonight.

I got my clothes washed so I'll add a few lines. I can't think of much to say. All I can do is send you my love. I guess I had better close for now.

Love
Bert

[He writes inside the gummed flap of the envelope]

"A kiss to the swellest girl in the world.
"Kathryn Kimzey"

Elbert D. Judkins S2/C
G.M. School Barracks 8-L
Camp Peterson U.S.N.T.S.
Farragut, Idaho
July 17, 1943

Dearest Kitty,
So two more letters get there the same day. I can't understand this mail myself. You really don't owe any letters and you answer better than anyone I know.

I'm sure glad you love to be a soda jerk, but I really hate to see you work at night, but you are one to trust. If you go with anybody take some brotherly advice and make darn sure you go out with the right guy. Don't think because I really think the world of you that I expect you to sit at home and become a woman because I want to see you really have fun. You know really I am being truthful. I don't have any use for a soldier. The majority don't care for nothing.

Yes I heard all about what was happening back in Indianola. I guess someone must be crazy. I guess the sheriff arrested several of the boys for stealing.

Really, I am getting to where I can't sit still long enough to write. I have a buddy that is always nagging at me to go somewhere. He's from St. Paul, Minn., and he's a swell guy. He hardly says very much but last night I got a little life history out of him. He has a brother in the Navy that was reported missing in action about a month ago. He is seventeen and his brother 21. That is why he's in the Navy today, to get revenge. He really is a swell boy. He would do anything for me. At the present he has gone to the school building to find out my pay number and how much money I have coming. I haven't been paid the last pay day and I hope I get a fair sum this time, which is Monday.

You know I expect the folks back home think I'm spending money foolish but I'm not. I get $54 a month, my insurance comes out and I signed for bonds. The highest I ever drew was $50. And that was just before I went on leave and I wasn't drawing my full check.

I still didn't raise my grades in school much. If I get a rate it will only be on my good looks, ha! I guess all I can do is try. There are a few too many boys here with college credits for me to get anywhere.

Tomorrow is Sunday. I plan on sleeping blame late in the morning but I expect some sap will roll me out of bed. He wants to look out if he does because I might get mad. That sure hurts me to have to control my temper. Too many of these boys are overbearing.

Gee, but it is dusty and dirty here now. They are talking about changing the uniform to whites. I hope they don't because it would mean washing every night.

Say, Kitty, I went outside to smoke and left my letters laying here. Someone has borrowed them. If you get a letter don't think I gave anyone your address. That is the last thing I would dare do.

If I ever lay hands on anyone looking over my things, oh boy. I guess I'm careless. I expect my wrist watch will be next. I broke it and I leave it in my dress jumper under my mattress.

I don't believe I told you about the trouble I had at home with a boy. He was going to clean me but he didn't try it for some reason. I expect he had an idea I was seeing a little training.

We went over the Commando Course today. I hit my leg on a fence and don't think I don't have a knot on it. I've seen plenty of boys go out on it just because they exerted theirself.

Well, sweetheart, I believe this will do for awhile. I'll write every time I have time.

Lots of Love and Kisses
Bert

Elbert D. Judkins S2/C
G.M. School Barracks 8-L
Camp Peterson U.S.N.T.S.
Farragut, Idaho
July 22, 1943

My Dearest Sweetheart,

I'm just a little slow in writing to my girl but maybe you won't mind too bad. I wish I would get some mail. I haven't heard from you for several days. It just takes five days for me to get a letter from you.

Gee, but I'm so blame tired tonight. This morning they came over here to get two volunteers for K.P. works. The way they picked them was you and you and I happened to be one they pointed at. I worked from five till 6:30 tonight. I was doing about everything but I sure got filled with oranges and pies. I know I ate two pies anyway.

School is still going but ever so slow. They are really rushing us through. The way we are going they may cut us short a month sooner. I hope so.

The weather here has been rather warm the last few days. I guess it can get hot but it cools off at night so it really isn't so bad for sleeping.

It happened today that I ran into a boy from Lacona, Iowa. I knew him well, he's a darn swell boy too. We had quite a chat together about different kids at home. I also ran into a fellow that knew a girl in Indianola by the name of Pat Rushing. Do you know her? I think I do but not for certain.

I guess about Sunday is a certain good looking girl's birthday. I wish you a very happy one and I hope you don't feel too old. I guess I won't be able to get into town to send you a present so I will send you five dollars. You can buy whatever you wish. There really isn't anything nice enough for you.

I've sure got a lot of people I should write tonight but time is very short and I have to hit the bed early tonight for it is school tomorrow.

Well, sweet, I can't think of anymore to say so I guess I will close until I hear from you.

All the Love in the World
Elbert

Happy Sweet 16 Birthday to me. I don't remember what I bought with Bert's $5.00, but that is quite a sum for these days. War horror stories are rampant, rationing is worse every day. Hitler and the reports of his brutality and hostilities are in all of the headlines. Victory is on the far, far horizon. We know our sailor will be in the middle of action soon.

UNITED STATES NAVAL TRAINING STATION
FARRAGUT, IDAHO

July 25, 1943

Dearest Kitty,
I think I owe you about ten letters so I'll try and get one finished so I can mail it tonight.

I'm really getting sick of the place, if I may say so. To add a little more work now the uniform is white. Imagine what a person looks like when he marches to school in dust around his ankles.

I just got back from the lake a while ago. I was on a motor boat about all afternoon. I really had fun but when I came back I found out my buddy had been taken to the hospital. I haven't found out what's the matter.

I got a swell letter from Marcia today. She really writes to me a lot and they are swell letters. I like to get plenty of mail. Don't forget that.

Do you hear from Kendall any more? I sure hope he gets his furlough.

That darn Lavare Cornell was down to see me tonight. He gets another leave. Some guys are plain lucky. He just had one the same time as I.

Gee! But it is ever so hot here now. I hope it rains so it will cool off. It is too hard to stay awake in school when it's this way.

A chief just stepped in and broke up a fight in here. He also said for us to get in bed pretty quick so I'll have to cut this short.

Are you working awful hard these days? Kitty, I'd give the world to see you. Really, you don't know how much I think of you. I think of you all the time even though I don't write often.

> *All the Love in the World*
> *Bert J.*

His letters sound a little like they are written by a young kid away in summer camp for the first time. I can read between the lines and I know how worried and depressed and unhappy he really is.

UNITED STATES NAVAL TRAINING STATION
FARRAGUT, IDAHO

July 27, 1943

My Dearest Sweetheart,
I don't suppose this letter will make sense with all the noise going on but I'll do my best on it.

The weather here is terrible hot. It is a little cooler since we changed the uniform to whites but it still doesn't agree with me.

Well, it won't be too many weeks till you start to school again, will it? I hope you like it. I expect it will be somewhat harder than Indianola but I won't be there to keep you from studying at nights so maybe you can get it. I hope you don't have another boy to keep you out at nights. These nights are hard on CHILDREN!

I got a swell letter from George today. He is really working now. He thinks Kendall will be sent to Colorado. It would make him a little closer home, I guess. Maybe his folks can go and see him.

George still has his mind on enlisting. A very foolish guy. He's just like the rest of these squirts that are seventeen. No kidding, they do us more dirt than good. They came in for pleasure and then they get down-hearted and don't care for nothing after this. They are always gumming things up for the rest. We have several boys here that young and they are always getting into trouble.

I got a letter from Homer. He's in Guadalcanal and he's really homesick. Boy, I don't have a thing to complain about here after what those boys go through with. So much for the troubles.

Is your dad still planning on coming to California? It would be swell if he would. I'll bet a certain girl hopes so.

At the present we have a short vacation every evening. That is what it seems like anyway considering the hours we did have. We get off at 15 minutes after four and go to bed at 10 so I have time to study and write a few letters. Well I've ran out of notes so will quit.

Loads of Love and Kisses,
Bert

Bert is writing about all of his friends at home, but he never mentions the best friend of all, Merle Curnes. They grew up together and were inseparable in the small farm community of Liberty Center, Iowa. They went to school, and hunted and worked together. A small shack was built on the corner of a cornfield on Bert's family farm. The two of them lived there at times. It held a stove, beds and food, and their precious dogs. They became blood brothers there after cutting their fingers with a dirty knife and pressing the wounds together. Why doesn't he mention Merle. Is it too painful to do so?

Elbert D. Judkins S2/C
G.M. School Barracks 8-L
Camp Peterson U.S.N.T.S.
Farragut, Idaho
July 31, 1943

Dearest Kathryn,

I finally got the long-awaited letters. I've waited a week for this letter. Every day I kept thinking I'd hear from you but nothing doing. I guess you don't know what those letters from L.A. mean. Don't take the bawling out too serious. I know you are busy but I would like to hear at least twice a week.

I'm sure glad you had a swell time on your birthday. I thought of you but that is all the good it done. I think of you every night but I guess there are several miles between us at present.

You said you were going to have your picture taken. I don't know of anything I would rather have. By the way, I would lots rather have a large one but I don't know, I don't have a very good place to keep it so maybe you had better send me a small, that is if they aren't right little ones like the ones I carry in my billfold. I would rather have them bigger.

By the way, what did you mean you have lots of things to say that you can't tell me in a letter. Surely you can tell ME!

Talk about heat, it is getting plenty hot here and how the dust blows. It is awful. I put on a clean pair of whites tonight and went to ships service for writing paper and now they are black. It is really hard to keep clean here.

We went to the rifle range today for a little target practice. It was sure the berries marching to and from there. I guess I'm disgusted with the weather.

I think I will be leaving here in eight more weeks. I have a pretty good idea what I will be doing but I won't say until I'm sure. They have cut out on some of the schooling and am I glad.

At present I have a black eye. It is really a shiner too. It is the first one I've packed for a long time. I got it boxing and the worst of it is the other guy has nothing at all.

Well of a night when I should be able to catch up on sleep I have to draw a guard watch. It is only two hours but I really hate to get up at 12 and go back to bed at 2. I guess I will live through with it. I always have.

Well, to get back to letter writing. I just had a hot quarrel with three California boys. We went around and around but only in words. I don't know why but they really think they are someone. When they bring Iowa into anything then I get mad.

I got a letter from sis today. I guess Atha has really been sick. They didn't think she would live for a while. She had pneumonia. I guess she's O.K. now.

Well, I'm out of news so I expect I had better sign off for now. Write.

Lots of Love,
Bert

"S.M.R.L.H." is written on the back of the envelope. What does this mean? [Editor's note: "S.M.R.L.H." meant "Sailor's (or Soldier's) Mail, Rush Like Hell".]

Chapter 9

Elbert D, Judkins S2/C
G.M. School Brks 2-Lower
Camp Peterson U.S.N.T.S.
Farragut, Idaho
8/3/43

Dearest Kitty,
    Not much to write about but I'll let you know I'm thinking of you.
    I'm ever so busy these weeks. Worse than ever before. School gets tougher and tougher as the days go on and of course I get lazier and lazier.
    Well I've changed locations again. We moved to barracks two. Too tough for the electricians I guess. All you need to do in writing me is to change the barracks number to 2.
    The other night as I was writing you my buddy slipped up behind me and took your address down. Yesterday he wrote you a letter but it so happened I got a letter from my cousin in California and I showed him the address and said that you had moved. He then let me read the letter. Oh! Boy, I'd sure hated for you to have gotten it because he can really flatter the girls. He's a swell guy but I don't trust these guys with my girlfriend.
    [I still think it sounds like the "boys" are in summer camp instead of the military, preparing to go who-knows-where to fight a terrible war. They are so young and inexperienced.]
    Well, my day's work has ended so I'll finish my letter. I just got back from the commando course. I really got fooled on it tonight. I had to really run it and make every object. They had guards posted

all the way around it and even took the names down as you made the objects. I guess they don't want any slackers.

Tonight I met another boy here that has my name. He's in the same barracks but on the top side. I guess he came from Missouri. I don't suppose he's any relation but I really don't know.

You say it is awful hot down there. It gets plenty cold here of a morning. You remember how my teeth used to chatter as we walked home from the show? They do that every morning here. I'll bet the snow is flying before I leave here. I sure hope not. Winter here is worse than Iowa, I guess.

No mail again today. I'd sure like to know where my mail is going. These letters mean a lot to me. Yesterday a boy I knew in barracks 5 brought a letter to me from Winnie. I guess I'm newsed out again so will bring this to a close.

Love and Kisses
Elbert

Elbert D. Judkins S 2/C
G. M. School Barracks 8-Lower
Camp Peterson U.S.N.T.S.
Farragut, Idaho
Aug. 1, 1943

Dearest Kitty,

Since I'm in the mood I'll drop a few lines to L.A. I've really spent a wonderful Sunday today.

This morning I went on guard at twelve till two then I got up at six and went to breakfast. After breakfast Lavare Cornell and Bob Hutchcroft came down. We sat around and talked over various things. They are supposed to go out on a gunners mate draft soon. I expect they will be sent right here. Lavare was supposed to get a leave but it was canceled. He was sure mad. He even had his leave papers made out.

Was I ever mad this afternoon. I was taking a nap and I had a dream. I was back home and you were there. That's all I can remember. It seemed so real and then I woke up still here. I could have screamed. I've slept from 12 till 4 o'clock this eve.

Yesterday we went on the rifle range. When we came back we were sitting around talking when a officer came in. My pal and another boy forgot to salute him. They go to mast right away. We sure have to be ever so careful. This is the way they select their men for rates. The ones with the best records on behavior and also their grade.

Tomorrow I start the fifth week of my school. Time really flies. Not many more weeks to go but I sure hate to roll out and take exercises.

These boys here have the radio going full speed. I can't even hear myself think. They are listening to the program "Farragut Calling". It comes on between 8 and 8:15 every Sunday night. It's a short program and it's pretty good.

My arms are really sore. Anyone that ducks a hit here receives five punches on the shoulder just as hard as they can hit. This evening I've got my share. They get pretty rough around here at times.

On the top side of this barracks are electricians. Last night after Taps they were stamping on the floor to keep us awake. It about started a free for all. They won't let us play push ball against them anymore. We play rough.

Well, sweet, I've been at this letter for about an hour and still I haven't said anything so I'll sign off with

Lots and Lots of Love and Kisses
Bert

P.S. I'll be looking for the picture. Don't forget you have a boyfriend here. Tell Richard and your Mom hi for me.

USO E.D.   *Judkins S2/C*
G.M.School Barracks 2 lower

U.S.N.T.S.
Farragut, Idaho
Aug. 8, 1943

Dearest Kitty,

I expect it is about time I drop you a line.

I came into Sandpoint this morning to just relax and forget about school. I'm about fed up on school but they won't let me out. I want to leave. I don't care where but I'm tired of this. They sure are working us.

They have a Commando Course here and always before I knew several shortcuts and never really run it so now they have guards on it and you have to run it. I guess it is for our own good but it's work.

The other morning we failed to get up for exercises. As a result we run on the drill field for two hours. First we would run and then walk. I was sure tired when our time was up.

This is sure a swell place here in Sandpoint. The people are so friendly. The USO is really swell. They have about everything to do.

I haven't heard from you for sometime and no word from home for two weeks. I suppose you are still a waiter.

When does your school start? Gee, you really don't know how bad I want to come to California. I expect it will be three months longer before I leave here but time really flies.

You know I've never gone with a girl out here and what's more I don't aim to. I'm absolutely leaving them alone.

Well, honey, this isn't a very long letter but no more to write about.

Lots and Lots of <u>LOVE</u>
Bert

S2/C Elbert D. Judkins
G.M.School Brks. 2 Lower
Camp Peterson
U.S.N.G.M.S.
Farragut, Idaho
August 9, 1943

My Dearest Kitty,

I don't have anything to do between now and bed so I'll try and get a few letters in the mail. This probably won't make sense, with the radio full blast and the rest of the noise.

You say you are about to die from the heat and here I am about to freeze. I Happen to have two blankets on my bed every night. I stand around every morning and really shake. It won't be long till winter will start here. I sure hope I'm gone by then.

This is sure the berries. I borrow paper to write you a letter and on the box is your address. It is a wonder you aren't getting some letters. These guys have all my addresses now.

I gave your address to my buddy last Friday. You see I was called up for an operation but got out of it. I was sure scared for a while. I guess it wasn't much or they would have kept me. I don't know what it was but they turned me loose and I'm not going back.

I sure hope the kids down there aren't like the boys here. You see, I don't think much of them but they are mates I guess. I'm sure glad you like it there. I hope I'm there but it is very certain I won't be there for long.

I'm pretty sure I won't even come out rated but that really doesn't make any difference to me. I have a very good idea what I'm going to do and I could be leaving here most any time but I expect it will be a while yet.

Say, Miss, the way you sound, you talk as if you thought I may not want you for a girlfriend when I get back. Don't fool yourself. I'll always want you. I haven't as much as looked at a girl here. I won't take these girls out around this place by all means.

I went into Sandpoint Sunday. I had to be back at 10 O'clock Sunday night and all the buses were loaded. I and six other boys brought a cab back. Boy, it sure cost some money. Anything is better than Capt. Mast. I don't aim to ever be A.O.L. I don't like the looks of being on K.P.

Well, Sweetheart, I haven't said much but just remember I love you and always will.

Lots of Love
Bert

P.S. What is Richard doing? Tell the folks hi for me.

[What a sweet boy he is. He has no idea what his life will be like soon, so young and inexperienced in life. The terrible war is going to last for a long, long time.]

Elbert D. Judkins S2/C
G.M. School Barracks 2-L
Camp Peterson
Aug 15, 1943

Dearest Kitty,

Sunday, boy, that day really means a lot to me. One day out of seven that I can spend the day as I wish.

Well, I hope this letter finds you in the best of health. I haven't gotten a letter from you all week. You must be terribly busy now. I can well understand what work is. I'm very busy myself. I always find something to keep me busy. Through the week it's study. Many of the boys go to night school but I don't seem to be that interested myself.

What are you doing to keep yourself busy? Are you still a soda jerk? I wish I were down there to spend the afternoon with you. Gee, I'd give the world to be there.

I'm still looking forward to leaving from California. I sure hope I do. I don't know how much more school I have but not too much, I hope. I want to leave here before winter. It gets awful cold here, I guess.

By the way, I was offered a special liberty and turned it down. Can you feature that? These towns here aren't nothing. They don't have much doing in them.

Boy, are they ever getting stiff in this camp. It is by far worse than boot camp. The only difference is I don't wear boots only on guard duty.

I said I was going to get a day at peace but I see I have to go on guard from 4:30 till 7 o'clock tonight. I guess that isn't so long but I'd much rather write letters.

The folks back home don't even write anymore. I can't blame them a whole lot because I don't write them very often. I don't have the time. I haven't gotten a letter from Theo's since I came back. I shouldn't even write them but I'd better, I guess.

Well, sweet, I'm not very good at letter writing anymore so I will sign off with

Lots of Love and Kisses
Bert

Elbert D. Judkins S/C
G.M. School Barracks 2-Lower
Camp Peterson U.S.N.T.S.
Farragut, Idaho
Aug 16, 1943

My Dearest Kitty,
Say, I've begun to think someone has forgotten me. What is the matter, are you awfully busy? Please write more often. Really, there is nothing I would rather get than a letter from you.

I've got the blues tonight. I'm one disgusted guy. They have really cracked down on us. This is really heck here if it ever was. Why unload troubles on you?

Well, back to letter writing. Us boys have been arguing about states again. California and Iowa, that is about all this station is made of.

I sure played heck last week for a chance for a rate. My average sure dropped. Didn't work hard enough I guess or maybe I didn't care. All I'm waiting for is to go to sea and as soon as possible. School is too tough for this guy and besides, I don't like it.

I never even went into town this week. There isn't anything to do but walk the streets and get tired so I stayed here and wrote letters and slept. I received a return letter today that I wrote to George June 23.

Say, I had a little piece in the county paper I had a notion to send you about Alfred Onstot and then I decided different. I was afraid you might write him, Ha! By the way, Miss Killam won't write me anymore. She has never written since I was back there. I guess she didn't approve of me going with the girls while I was there. I went with three different girls. Two were engaged, so what? I was just a sailor to them.

If I had my life to live over I'm afraid things would be different. One thing for sure, I would have stayed with Kendall. I guess I made a mistake and no way to change. No one can ever tell me anything that would change my mind. I have a lot of pals here and a good many that I don't think anything of.

Well, sweetheart, I need some sleep as I went to sleep twice in school today and had to be wakened.

Love
Bert

Tuesday morning. I never got the letter mailed last night so will add a few lines. I feel somewhat better this morning and I'm hoping to hear from you today.

Last night while I was looking at the county paper I ran onto the sketch about Dick Downey. That was Dory's brother, wasn't it? I thought it was but wasn't sure. He was in Guadalcanal, a gunner on a bomber. [He was killed in a plane crash. He was the brother of a good friend of mine.] *That is why Homer ran onto him.* [Brother Homer was in Guadalcanal as well.]

Well, Miss, I'll seal this letter this time and with a great big kiss. Are you still bashful with your kisses? Ha!

All the Love in the World
Bert

Elbert D. Judkins S2/C
G.M. School Barracks 2-lower
Camp Peterson U.S.N.T.S.
Farragut, Idaho
Aug 17, 1943

Dearest Kitty,

I don't have a whole lot to write about as I just sent a letter to you this morning but at least I can answer your letter that I finally got today.

Oh! Well, I'll forgive you this time but don't let it happen again because I do like to hear from you even if you don't like to write.

Well, there hasn't been anything interesting happen here either but don't you worry there has been plenty going on.

I inquired about getting out of school but nothing doing. I can take it, I hope. I asked for anything but here I am. I guess I can stand it 9 more weeks.

You asked me when I got to leave here. I only wish I knew. I hope I get to come down but don't look too strong. I've been disappointed before. You can't tell where you will go. Say, Miss, I know you don't want to see me half as bad as I do you. I'm just a little bit afraid that I'll leave from someplace else but don't know.

The letter I got today from you was mailed the 13th. It was the first letter I've gotten from you for about 2 weeks but I still forgive you. You see, I haven't heard from the folks for some time and I have never heard from Theo's since I came back.

Well, sweet, I've got a lot of studying to do between 7:30 and 9 so must close. Write soon, please.

Love, Bert

S2/C Elbert D. Judkins
G.M. School Barracks 2-L
Camp Peterson
Aug. 22, 1943

Dearest Kitty,

I'm going to have to stop letter writing pretty soon now but I'll take time to write <u>you</u>. I haven't heard from you for sometime.

I keep looking forward to the next day but still no letters.

I got a letter from Barbara Jean. She sure bawled me out for not writing her so I did today.

I went into town Saturday. There wasn't anything there so I got a room and slept till 12 O'clock today. I really enjoyed that. My buddy and I got into a quarrel. I don't know what it started about but I got hot and told him off so I went into town by myself. It was by far the best thing that could have happened to me.

Listen, Kathryn, why don't you forget me? I'm serious. I don't believe I'm good enough for you.

You know when I was home it was different but now it isn't. I'm being truthful. I forgot about drinking once and I'm trying to now but it seems like there is always someone egging you on. I've never been off the base but what I've taken a drink so you see what I mean. I believe in telling the truth. You're the swellest girl I ever knew but I'm not the swellest boy, so forget me. Just remember this, be careful who you go with because they aren't all like me.

Well, I guess I've said enough. Don't be too mad, I still think the same of you and I don't exactly want you to hate me.

Love
Bert

He doesn't know me very well if he thinks I will forget him this easily. I decided a long time ago he was my man, and I meant it. He is so depressed and homesick, I will be patient with him. He deserves a drink or two now and then.

He must have forgotten he asked me to forget him just the other day. I received the following just three days later.

Elbert D. Judkins S2/C
G.M.School Barracks 2-Lower
Camp Peterson U.S.N.T.S.
Farragut, Idaho
Aug. 28, 1943

Hi Sweet,

While I'm in a good mood, maybe I had better drop you a few lines. This has been a pretty decent Saturday considering that I stood out on the drill field all morning for personal inspection. At least I've had the afternoon off.

So you are quitting your job for a vacation. Good enough, I would too if I were you. You know if I were at home I'd be out every night (that I wasn't sleeping.)

School starts the 13th. Are you glad or do you wish summer was longer? Here I'm wishing I were out of school. Someday I'll wish I were back in, I know. Oh, well, it can't last much longer but I hate to think of those next 8 weeks. I'll have so much to learn.

By this time I expect Marilyn and your Aunt Euna are there. Tell them hello for me.

So you are still hoping I get sent down there. If you really want to see me bad to keep from disappointing you it is very doubtful whether I'll ever land near L.A. You see they have something else in line for us boys and I expect we will leave farther north. One never knows for sure though and a lot can happen between now and then.

I could call you but I've lost every one of my addresses, including your phone number.

Now to get back to letter writing. I've been outside blowing with the boys about our grades in school. For some reason I don't seem to be getting along so good. I'm going to have to work harder, I guess.

Well, Kitty, this is very short but really I can't think of anything to write about.

Lots of Love and Kisses
Bert

Elbert D. Judkins S2/C
G.M. School Barracks 2-Lower
Camp Peterson U.S.N.T.S.
Farragut, Idaho
Aug. 25, 1943

Dearest Kitty,

I expect by the time you receive this letter you won't think very much of me and I don't blame you but I'm still going to write you until you tell me to stop.

I got two letters from you today. One was mailed the 9th, the other the 21st. I was ever so surprised to hear from you but was very glad to get them.

I finally heard from Carolyn K. I guess the girls went camping at the lake for a week. They seemed to have a lot of fun.

I knew that the kids in Indianola would tell you everything that went on so the last letter I wrote I told you to forget me but surely we can still be pals. I'm not mad at you. I have no reason to be, but you do.

Boy, am I in a hurry to get out of here. My nerves are about no nerves. I'm continually flying off the handle to everyone. I've tried every way there is to get out but all is in vain. I even volunteered for naval commandos but I'm still here and will be for 8 more weeks.

I guess all your folks will be in California before long. That's swell. Is Marilyn going to school there this fall?

You say you are having a lot of fun there. I expect there are a good many things to do. It's sure different here. I'm 45 miles from the nearest town. In it there are 2 theaters with no new shows. There are plenty of taverns and girls but no decent girls, just a bunch of ignorant ones that ought to be put to bed yet and the town is full of sailors. What is there for a person to do? After I leave here maybe I'll see how civilized people live once again. I'm not going to town anymore. I must save money to leave on.

Every letter you've asked when I was coming down. Well, I don't know for certain but it is very likely. I hope so before winter. I sure don't want to stay here this winter.

I saw in the Des Moines paper where a boy that went through boots with me was missing in action. He was a swell guy. Maybe I told you about him before. He lived in Des Moines and was only 17. He was engaged while he was home. I met his girlfriend the night we came back. I hope he's just missing. [Editor's note: This is apparently a reference to Edwin Prothero, mentioned in Elbert's letter of June 26, 1943. Mr. Prothero eventually made it back to Des Moines at some point in his life. The circumstances surrounding his disappearance are unknown, but he would one day have a grandson, also named Edwin Prothero. We have been in contact with the younger Prothero. His grandfather is no longer alive, and he never met him. He knew nothing about his ever being missing in action.]

I also got a letter from Homer. That guy thinks I'm a kid, I guess. If he knew what I was really going through with he'd stop worrying. They don't have kids here.

While blowing I saw a boy in boots only 14 years old. He asked us boys how hard it was for a person that young to get out. The younger and older ones just can't keep up.

We do a lot of crabbing for things we do such as wash <u>windows</u> but it wouldn't be the Navy if we never.

Signing off now as it is 8:30 and I have a pile of clothes to get off the line before someone steals them.

Love
Bert

Chapter 10

Dearest Sweet,

My morale is pretty fair today since I received the swell pictures. Gee, but they sure make me homesick to see you. I've seen a lot of girls but none compare with you. In fact you're too swell. I've showed those pictures to all the boys here and do they think you are good looking.

No, I can't say Mary Jo looks like you. She's better looking, ha! Does that make you mad? She sure is a doll.

Well 9 weeks of school has passed and that is 9 too many. I'll bet if I knew a few things I'd be to sea now.

I've been outside shooting off again. About all I get done is blow about Iowa. I guess there isn't much back there now though.

So you dread starting to school among strangers. Think how many I've met and then the best leave. That is one thing I hate. You meet someone swell and hope you can stay with him and then you part.

I showed the pictures to a boy from L.A. He recognized the place you were standing by Hank.

Say, the way you sound, you really do think some of me. No kidding, I've not been raising near as much Cain as I expect it sounded in my letter.

Today was liberty for me but I never cared to go into town. I was afraid I wouldn't come back, ha! Up here I don't even know which way is which so I wouldn't get far.

I got a letter from Lina last week stating that Fred was a Marine and was headed for San Diego. The lucky stiff. I guess most of the boys have me bested.

Hon, I think you are counting too much on me coming to California. I'll tell you my chances, all rated men go to an advance school down there. Non-rated go straight to sea. I'm afraid I'm one of the non-rated, the way it looks. I'll tell you why if I see you.

The uniform of the day has been changed for fall weather and we've even been wearing our overcoats, so you see it is getting colder all the time. I'm sure in a hurry to leave here before the snow starts. I guess it gets plenty deep here.

You sure can write swell letters. Can't you give me a few pointers? I'm not doing so good lately. I haven't written home for so long I expect they wonder if I'm still here. I might surprise them and write tomorrow.

You finally say something about Dick. I had begun to wonder if he were there with you. Ask him when he is going to join the Navy and be with me. Tell him he could learn to shoot a gun a trifle bigger than his air rifle. I believe these would kill a rabbit too. We could have a pretty good time here.

Every one of these boys in this section have tattoos on them. So far I haven't had the nerve to get one put on me and I guess maybe I won't.

Sometime ago I got a letter from Homer. He said he wrote my name on one of the bombs he dropped the other night. He's just a trifle proud of his little brother the way he sounds but he still thinks I'm a kid. Maybe I am, I don't know. I feel like an old man though. I have to work too hard, ha! No, I really don't work as hard as I did at home but I'm busy more now. Here you wait too much.

Sometime ago I got a letter from Miss Nine at Indianola saying that some of the boys were caught selling gas coupons and they were given the choice of the pen or the army. You know Francelia Nine don't you? A little girl I believe you were jealous of. Well, she's engaged now. I guess about all of them are wearing rings. These guys here think I ought to be where I could watch you. They say someone will steal you sure as heck. Will they?

Well, "babe," I've written about all I know of so I guess I'll have to bring this thing to a close. I hope to hear from you soon and I'd better or OH! Boy!

Lots and Lots and Lots of Love and Kisses
Bert

Elbert D. Judkins S2/C
G.M.School Barracks 2 lower
Camp Peterson
USNTS Farragut, Idaho
Sat. Sept. 6, 1943

Dearest Kitty,
   You can give me heck this time for not writing but the same old excuse, "busy."
   I guess us boys have been raising too much heck because we've even had to work after dark, which is very unusual. They put me on a 5 hour watch Thursday night then school Friday. Work Friday night till 8 then work today. I guess maybe we'll have tomorrow off.
   I've never hated anything like I hate this place. Imagine if anyone fails to put our proper address on the envelope we get put on report. I mean that is discipline. Oh! Well, I guess I'll meet with worse things.
   I did get a letter from Homer yesterday. He's a Lt. J.G. in the Navy now. [Navy? Homer is in the Army Air Force.] *He told me all about the place he was and what he was doing. He's shot down a Jap Zero or two and one sub.*
   Boy, I was kinda worried about Winnie. I went up and had the Red Cross see how serious she was. I guess she is coming along O.K. now.
   So you got to see some of the zoot-suiters work on the sailors and soldiers. I'll bet they never hurt the <u>sailors</u> any.

[Mother, Dick and I were in Lowes State Theater in downtown Los Angeles watching a movie one evening when suddenly someone yelled, "Get the sailors!" The movie stopped playing, and the theatre lights were turned on. The zoot suit gang riots were rampant at that time in the city. Gangs of Latinos wearing the baggy trousers and long jackets and wide brim hats ran through the downstairs audience, jumping over seats and they fought with anyone wearing a uniform. Mass chaos erupted down there. We were seated in the balcony and could see everything below. Mother said, "Let's get out of here," and we made a hasty exit through the first door we saw. I was a little disappointed. I wanted to watch the fight!]

I don't know for certain when I'll leave here but next month sometime. I don't know where I'll go but I have a idea what I'll do. I think I'll get 2 months training in California. Or Maryland for the Navy "landing forces" but this isn't certain yet.

No, honey, I don't believe it would have done you any good to have tried and phone me. I don't expect they could have found me. I promise faithfully I'll call you if I don't get down there anywhere.

I sure have a sore shoulder on me. I was out on the rifle range one day this week and I couldn't hit the target half the time. When a guy really wants to do something he can't do it. I flunked my test this week and then couldn't qualify on the range. A heck of a guy I am.

[This is unusual for Bert, he has been known all of his life at home for being a sharpshooter. He won every contest he entered.]

Well, sweetheart, I can't think of any more to say so will close.

Love, Bert

Elbert D Judkins S2/C
G.M. School
Barracks 2-Lower
Camp Peterson USNTS
Farragut, Idaho
Sept 6, 1943

My Dearest Sweetheart,
While I'm killing time I just as well drop you a line.

I just got a letter from George. He's quitting school. I guess he knows what he's doing but he is rather foolish, I think. He said Kendall was coming home on a furlough. I'm glad of that.

I never had to go to school today but I had to work. I went around cleaning furnaces and I mean I was simply black when I came back. I sure had a job scrubbing clothes.

I felt sure I'd get a letter from you today but no. I guess you don't love me anymore. Ha! That's what I tell the boys every time I fail to hear from you.

It begins to look like I'm going to spend part of the winter here. Right now I have a sweater on. I gotta keep warm somehow. I could stand the cold if I were back home walking home with you or out coasting. I didn't mind it at all then. I wonder why.

Now to get back to letter writing. I just returned from chow and I mean it wasn't a feast tonight. Pretty poor for a hungry boy.

I expect by this time you have started your first day of school. Well I hope you never met a good looking boy that might be heck for me. By the look at the pictures it wouldn't pay for you to meet someone handsome. Those pictures were sure swell and don't think I wasn't proud of them. I'd give a whole lot to see you all again. I guess all I can do is hope. Kitty, if you ever want a favor anyway or anything and I can help you, just let me know. I'd do the impossible for you, no kidding. I don't know but I guess you have me over a barrel.

Golly it is sure hard for me to think of anything to say. I'm getting plenty poor at letter writing. I guess there really isn't much happening here to write about.

Has your dad come out yet? I sure wish you could see the country around here. I used to think I'd like to visit in the mountains but if I just get to buy a one-way ticket out of here I'll really be a happy sailor.

The boys are at it again. I mean arguing among themselves. That is about all I hear in the barracks. I get along pretty fair considering the way I was in civilian life. Well, honey, I've got to do a little reviewing and get in bed. Don't forget you have a boyfriend in Farragut, so write me a line. I don't know who I love to hear from any worse.

Love and Kisses
Bert

XXXX
Writing them on paper isn't
Like the real McCoy though is it?

Remember the first time I kissed
You? Oh boy I won't forget. It was my happiest.

Sun. Sept. 12, 1943

Dearest Kitty,

Sunday is a day of rest so I'll drop you a line. It will probably be rather short.

I'm waiting here to press my clothes for school next week. You know they must look just so for inspection.

How is school by this time? I suppose you have met many new friends. I sure hope you like it O.K. School is the best part of a person's life. I never knew that before but now when I really need my school to refer to I don't have the necessary credits. Two things I need the worst is physics and algebra and I've had neither. I got by this week luckily, but I don't know about next. I guessed on most of my work and it so happened I guessed right. So much for school. I hate it.

I got a letter yesterday from home with rather bad news in it. Winnie I guess fell some way and cracked two ribs and punctured a lung. I guess she isn't serious but they probably wouldn't tell me if she was.

Does Dick go to the same school as you? I'll bet he is having the time of his life out here.

It looks very doubtful whether I'll get home again or not. I really don't care if I can go to California.

I expect by this time Kendall is home. I'll bet Velma is glad. I sure wouldn't trade places with him but I would trade with my nephew. I wish I were a Marine now, although their training is plenty stiff. I'll bet he will wish he wasn't though. These "kids" don't know what they do want.

No kidding, I guess they have me where they want me. I don't fear nothing. They drill you and pound at your brain till you do things without thinking.

Last week our smoking was taken from us. Boy, I about went crazy for a while but we have it back now so I'll live.

I also got a letter from Bob Crabb. He's in San Diego. He of course told me all about it and said he was going over to L.A. to see some kids he knew.

Dinner is over so I'll get busy and finish this letter. We had a pretty fair meal but it don't compare with your mom's cooking that I ate in Indianola.

No mail again today. I can't understand it. I suppose everyone is busy at something.

I'm sure sleepy. I guess I'll take a little nap when I complete your letter. I've got to write George also. He never started back to school this year either.

It won't be much longer now till I'll be leaving. One more month. It sure won't be too soon for me. Some of the boys got to sign up for their next base. I hope I do. I'll come to Diego for sure then. I'm praying for it.

I got a letter from Barbara Jean last week. She sure gave me heck for not writing her but if they only knew how busy I really was.

Say, take notice of my address. Address all my letters like that. Some new orders, I guess.

Elbert D. Judkins S2/C
G.M.School Section 14
Barracks 2 Lower
Camp Peterson
U.S.N.T.S.
Farragut, Idaho

That address about covers a page.

I guess I had better sign off and I hope I hear from you soon even though you must be awfully busy.

All the love in the world,
Bert

Wed. Sept 15

Dearest Kitty,

This is the second letter I've started to you and I hope I get this finished.

Last night I started one and then decided to take a shower before the water got cold. Well, I jumped under it and it so happened it was already cold so I jumped back and my feet flew out from under me. My head hit the floor and as a result I cut my head above my eye. I had to have a couple stitches taken but she's O.K. now.

Oh! This school it seems to drag on and on. I guess I'm too anxious to leave here. I never was in such a hurry to find a new home. And I guess it is home.

I should be studying now but I've lost all points of interest. I only got a 69 last week.

I got a letter from my Aunt tonight. She hasn't heard from me for a couple months so she thinks I've gone to sea. As busy as I am she'll just have to think for awhile.

Kitty, I got the swell picture of you. I have it right before me as I am writing. I'm afraid it wouldn't do for you to meet up with any of these boys here. They think you are pretty cute and so does another boy here, I.

How's school coming along? I hope you really like it. I wish I were going to school with you.

Well we had a little excitement tonight. A forest fire was started here but was put out sudden like.

Honey, my address has been made a little longer but don't have it out or I won't get it.

I guess I had better close and study a little. Thanks a whole lot for the pictures and write when you aren't too busy.

Love and Kisses
Bert

Sat. Night Sept. 18

Dearest Sweetheart,

I believe a week ago you said you were home alone. Tonight I'm not alone but I would rather be. Oh! I get so tired of staying here when I could go into town but there isn't a thing to do in there either.

You haven't wanted to see me half as bad as I've wanted to see you. If you really knew how much I thought of you.

Kitty, you said you had been talking a lot about the Navy and mainly because I was in it. Remember once when you didn't want me to enlist in the Navy? I wish I had listened to you now. The water kinda makes me wonder, ha!

Yes, I promise I'll call before I go to sea but I still have my fingers crossed hoping I'll see you.

Well, honey, I sure don't feel very happy tonight. Atha just wrote me that Winnie was much worse. Golly, I don't know what to do. If only I knew just what her condition was. I guess I'll go up and see about an emergency leave, although I doubt if I can get one. She said she had double pneumonia. I guess no one has heard from Homer for better than a month.

The question you asked me about, do I want you to go with anyone? The answer would be no, but Kitty, I think the world of you and it is entirely up to you to decide that question. Do the thing you think is best and I'm sure you will be right.

I did O.K. in school this week. My grades are much better than they were but I've worked a lot harder to. I guess I'll live through all the work though.

Well, I've started this page but I can't think of a thing to say so will have to stop.

Loads of Love and Kisses
Bert

U.S.N.T.S.
Farragut, Idaho
Sept 29, 1930
[Oops, 1930?]

Dearest Darling Honey,

How's my little black-headed doll tonight? I don't expect this will make sense as I have 3 boys sitting beside me and telling me what to write. They are swell guys. I don't expect I'll meet any better pals while I'm in the Navy.

I received your most welcomed letter today. I don't know who I'd rather get a letter from. I'm glad you think so much of school.

As for me, I flunked another test today. I guess I'm just plain <u>ignorant</u>. At least I can say one thing. I've got my grades honest and I'm glad of it only because I believe these others will get tripped up eventually.

They passed another rule here. Anyone caught wearing their hats on the side of their head get boat haircuts. Also all names but your own must be removed from your shirts. This costs me the price of 3 shirts because I was proud and have Iowa written on them.

Next week we start night school. Boy I'll go plain crazy then so you don't want to look for many letters.

While I think of it, Carolyn Killam and Barbara Jean say you owe them a letter. Maybe you should write. They're plenty peeved.

Not many more years till I'll know whether I get to see you or not. I'll sure be one disappointed sailor if I don't. I've been disappointed a lot though.

Did I ever tell you George has a car? I guess he's having a lot of fun. He said he thought Kendall was going to get discharged.

You know sometimes I wish I were out of here and then again I don't. I'll admit I'm dissatisfied. You see, when I came in I was filled with lies. It's nothing like they say.

When I march out on the grinder and hear shouts like people driving cows well, and then look at the mountains on four sides, I wish with all my heart to leave here. I'm one that can take it but I've seen many that haven't. I'll be leaving this barracks this week but address my mail the same. After this week we'll be waiting for our orders.

It is 5 minutes till Taps so I must close. Write, honey, if you aren't too busy.

All the Love in the World
Bert

Good night, sweetheart. I wish I could make life easier for you.

Chapter 11

Dearest Kitty,

I'm not in the mood for letter writing today but I should drop my sweetheart a <u>note</u>.

Not anymore happening up here than usual. No excitement just work and wondering.

I got a letter today from my buddy at sea. He made me feel pretty fair but I believe he would rather be here. I only know I wouldn't. Things sound pretty fair now.

I went on my last liberty here yesterday. I had a pretty fair time. I went in with two dandy fellows. One of them is from L.A. We got back at 4 o'clock this morning and had to get up at six. This is the first liberty I've had for two months. All we did was eat, eat, eat. It costs money but at least I got what I liked. I had plenty of milk to drink too. Take notice that it was <u>milk</u>.

I had to come back sober or else.

Well, I won't be here longer than 2 weeks and I mean that will soon fly past. I don't know as yet where I will go but the promise still goes I'll call if I'm not coming your way. I'd lot rather see you and taste some lipstick again.

So your dad hasn't come out yet. It begins to look like you would have to go get him. Gee! I'd hate to think about facing winter at home again. I've had it plenty lucky being up here where it was cool all summer. It was never terrible hot here.

We have personal inspection again this weekend. That is something to really dread. You have to stand so long and it completely wears me out.

I've sure been catching heck from home. Neglect of writing. OH! I hate to write letters. After I leave here they will be lucky if they ever hear from me. I'll have to have you write them from me, I guess.

Well, Kitty, I'm so anxious to see you. I really don't know what I'll do if I don't see you before I leave. My sisters believe I'm lying when I say I don't get a leave. They think I'm coming down there but I wasn't lying, I don't get a leave.

Well, honey, write me a line when you aren't too busy.

Love and Kisses
Elbert

U.S.N.T.S.
Farragut, Idaho
Oct 7, 1943

Dearest Kitty,

I received your letter today so I'll answer while I have some time.

Gee! Hon, I wish you did like school better. Boy, I know what it is to have to go. I never ever cared for it but I did have a lot of fun.

Yep, it's been about a year now since I met the good looking girl. We did have a lot of fun together, although I was jealous every time you were out of my sight. Say, do you realize it's been six months since I've seen you? I doubt if you would even know me. I'm a lot heavier than I was and heaven only knows it isn't from eating.

Oh! I'm so disgusted and anxious to leave here that I'm ready to go anywhere. Boy, I guess we will be sent every direction and to do about anything.

We moved again tonight and I mean in one <u>censored</u> of a place. [Editor's note: It appears that Bert "censored" this himself. Nothing is blanked out. It looks like he simply wrote and underlined the word, "censored," where the word, "hell," belongs.] *Right up above us are about 100 guys. Down here we have 115 men sleeping on cots and bunks. Anyway, we won't be here too long. We graduate next Friday but will lay around in O.G.U. for a week or maybe months.*

I got a letter from my nephew in Diego. He's about as disgusted as I but I'm sure glad he isn't here. At least it will be warm down there this winter and I guess the snow gets deep here. It's getting colder right along here but it is about time now.

I've sure been catching heck from home. The girls haven't heard from me for a while.

I got a letter from Winnie yesterday. She said they had been looking for me home. I had put in for a leave but cancelled it when she got better. I couldn't bear to think of coming back here to this confounded boot camp. I thought I was promoted once but a boot is by far better off than we. Oh, well, why cry? It isn't doing any good.

We had our section pictures taken. They weren't worth a darn. We spoiled them by being salty and not squaring our hats. I wanted to get some singles taken but couldn't arrange it. I've got to get some taken though.

We have Captains Inspection Saturday. Hope I can get out of standing it but afraid I can't.

Well, honey, I'm rather sleepy and I've got a hard day ahead of me. We go to school all day now and 2 hours night school beside the watches we stand so if you are unlucky you can lose a lot of sleep and this is one school where you can't sleep in.

Good night, sweet, and here's hoping you write soon.

> *Love and Kisses*
> *Your beloved*
> *Sailor*

(P.S. I wish I was)
This dry land
sailing isn't agreeing.
I've heard the truth about sea duty. It's no fun but you can at least smoke and don't have to go to Captains Mast every day.

> *Oct. 10, 1943*

Hi Honey,
I'm so behind in letter writing I don't know which way to start. I expect the girls are on their toes because it has been 2 weeks since I wrote to them.

What are you doing right now? It makes me wonder and wish. I don't expect there is a whole lot for a young girl to do from what I hear of that town.

While I think of it I got a letter from Carolyn Killiam yesterday. She's rather angry because you haven't written her. You had better write.

Honey, I got in one of those games that I swore I was off. I made $100. But it was still foolish. We may get delayed orders and I had my last dollar at stake. If I'd have lost I wouldn't have gone far but the way it was I still had no money.

Hey, I just read in the county paper where Helen Beck is married. Gee! I felt bad, ha! Oh, well, there shouldn't be any jealously now.

It's sure hard for me to think of anything to write. Lets see, Yes, we have 2 weeks school left yet. We were set back for some reason. I guess I shouldn't care. The more I know the more chances I'll have of coming back. If only I was from here I wouldn't care.

It simply poured last night and I had my blankets hanging out.

We had Captains Inspection Sat. I wasn't suppose to have to stand it but just to be a good little boy I did as a result I got called on my hair. It's suppose to be cut down to where it's only 2 inches long. Mines about 4. I got it cut in town so that's why.

Short and sweet but I can't think of any more.

Love and Kisses, Just a sailor
U.S.Naval Training Station
Farragut, Idaho
Oct 13, 1943

Dearest Kitty,

It's getting nearer and nearer till my school ends and still I have nothing to show for it. I guess I won't get an advancement. I really don't care <u>much</u>. Just 4 months for nothing and spent in Farragut besides.

I started a letter to you Monday and then never finished it. I just can't seem to settle down long enough to write. All I do is jump up, smoke, cuss and fly off the handle at everyone.

Kitty, we had our group picture taken and one of the boys started cutting the best pictures out, I got mine and will send it to you. Just *to let you see me in uniform. I'll get some good ones taken before I leave the <u>states</u>. They haven't sent us our orders but will next week.*

I have an idea what mine will be. I expect I'll be sent to Pleasanton, Calif., for about 8 weeks commando training. It may be the best I hope.

It's getting plenty cold here now. It's froze a night or so and the way it feels it will tonight. I hope it waits till I leave before it snows.

I hope you're coming along in school O.K. and like it fine. I wish I were going to school with you. If I could only see you, I have so much I would like to tell you. But I can't. It might hurt me if it were to be read by some <u>certains</u>.

I got a letter from H. Beck yesterday. She had to tell me she was married and all the news. I haven't heard from Theo's for about 1 ½ months and, boy, I'm not writing. In fact, I haven't written the girls for about 3 weeks. And again I'm not. I don't like this letter writing too hot. I have to be still and think too much and my brain is about wore out from studying, ha!

Oh! Well, I've got a lot to be thankful for. At least there's you. Kitty, I'm not kidding, if it weren't for you and the sisters, I'd try something but I won't. I've not been in very serious trouble and can't afford to take chances.

Well, honey, keep those letters coming. I expect when you read this you'll see why. I need a morale builder, don't you think?

> *All the Love in the*
> *World*
> *Bert*

The picture looks like a heck of a sailor. I'd rather the uniform be brown with wings on it, wouldn't you?

No, I would not rather have him in a brown uniform with wings. I am very proud of my darling sailor in his navy blue. And so is he.

Sun. Oct 17

Hi Honey,

I expect it is about time I drop you a line or you'll think I've forgotten you. That's something I'll never do.

Listen, Kitty, I heard we were going out pretty quick. Of course, it's not real sure who will go but I have a chance so don't think I've forgotten you if you don't hear from me. I think I'm going to Alaska.

Gee! Since I think of it, in case you move I won't know your address and I'll be leaving here the last of the week. Oh! Well you can write one of the girls at home. They will know it.

Oh! I'm so disgusted I could bawl. Everything has gone wrong the last few days.

I guess there won't be any stripes on my arm. That makes me mad too. I really thought I was good for one. I have better grades than a lot of boys. Just so me and my Iowa buddy can stay together is all I'm asking.

Today it is simply pouring outside. It won't be long till the snow will be flying and this boy hopes he's gone.

I can't think of a thing to write about, honey. I guess there isn't any use for you to look for me in California, although there's still a very slim chance.

Well, honey, I must close. Loads of love and kisses, Bert

Oct 22, 1943

Hi Kitty,

Well, the big day is over. I've finished school and still a S2/C.

That is a disgrace for me. I guess there is some pride in me but, believe me, not much.

Honey, I'm suppose to come to California, to Frisco, but I won't believe it till I'm there. Luck has been pretty much against me.

We'll hope.

Oh! It's terrible here now. It snowed yesterday and is at it again. I don't expect I'll be waiting here much longer. I hope not.

We've moved into O.G.U. and, believe me, we're living under terrible conditions.

Sweet, I hope I can see you but don't know what I'll be doing there. At least it won't be school. I won't take that again. They can brig me.

Boy, I'll bet someone has a time if they try to work me here.

I plan on laying around doing nothing.

Kid, don't get the idea I've been raising Cain because I haven't.

My grades weren't hot but they were better than some that got rates.

This is the truth. We had a leader that I disagreed with so no soap for me. You have to get along with everyone if you want to get places.

So help me, that guy is leaving with me. Someone is going to get a beating before we get there.

So you still don't like school. Have you found a place to move yet? I wish it would be Frisco.

Well, no more to say. Be good and

Lots of Love
Bert

Remember I still love you.

More disappointments for my sailor. It seems he gets more than his share. Perhaps if he tried harder and stayed out of trouble things would be better for him. There is no end in sight for the war. Conditions worsen around the world. Stories and news of horrors and atrocities are beginning to reach our shores. Many young lives are being sacrificed. I dread the terrible days ahead of us.

United States Naval Training Station

Farragut, Idaho

Oct 25, 1943

My Dearest Kitty,
They are making so much noise in this place I can't hear myself think but I'll attempt to drop you a note.

Oh! That letter I got from you and Vivian. It makes me wonder. I believe you have gone insane, ha.

Gee, I'm sleepy. That blankety-blank guard woke me up twice this morning and told me I was suppose to work. It finally came to an end and I didn't work. I'm not going to work either.

I have to laugh every time I look at this letter. Boy, it beats anything I ever saw.

Ahem! How good of a looker is Vivian. Will I ever find out? You had better not trust me too far. Remember you didn't used to. I'll never forget how mad you used to get once in awhile. Oh, well, I was the same way. Do you ever stay awake at night wondering what I'm doing? Ha. Well don't because I'm usually sleeping or walking a cursed post. There aren't any girls around these towns beautiful enough for me. I'm choicy. They have to be GOOD LOOKING.

Boy, that chicken dinner you spoke of sounded good. I don't know what chicken tastes like, just fish, fish and more fish. I hate them and I don't eat when they have them.

Hey, how are you going to explain the letter? I'll probably never receive the letter of explanation. Oh, well, I guess I can understand what 2 girls will do.

[We wrote to him on toilet paper! It accomplished its purpose, I think. It made him laugh.]

Hey, tell your girlfriend I have no use for a Marine. Maybe I shouldn't have said that. Oh, well, I still don't. I'm just a sailor so why should I voice my opinion?

I hear Neil is home. The lucky stiff. Boy what I wouldn't give for a 30 day leave or any amount for that matter. I can't see why I should lay around here. I WON'T work, that's final. I'm a old salt at Farragut, 7 months and never seen the sea.

I will in about 4 days from what I hear. My name is posted and it looks like some more training ahead of me. I guess I can take most anything. Just so it isn't here. I too would become insane then.

Honey, I guess there isn't any use to write me here any more.

I may leave tomorrow in place of Wednesday. I'll try to call you when I get to California. I'm going to San Francisco, I guess.

So long and be good.
Love and Kisses
Bert

Chapter 12

E.D. Judkins S2/C   *FREE*
Oakland, Calif.   *Buy*

WAR SAVINGS
BONDS and STAMPS

Miss Kathryn Kimzey
4326 South Harvard
Los Angeles 37
California

USO   *Nov. 5, 1943*

Hi Kitty,

Here I am in California. Just got in today. Don't know what I'm in for yet as I haven't gone to the base yet. I'm due out there tomorrow. I guess I'm still a long way from you, aren't I?

By the way, I've been home. I saw your dad. I believe he'll be out before long.

I expect you have been wondering what became of me, haven't you? I'm still alive and thank the Lord I've left Farragut. I had a fair time at home. I was only there 4 days. I saw Neil. We spent a night together talking over old times.

I had my pictures taken. The girls are supposed to send you one, so don't dun me for it.

I don't suppose I'll be here much longer. I hope not. I don't care especially for California.

I'm stationed about 40 miles from San Francisco. I don't know what it's like there.

Well, I'll tell you more tomorrow.

Bert

U.S.Navy
Personnel Distribution Center
Pleasanton, California

Elbert D. Judkins S 2/C
U.S.N.R.B.
Barracks 0222
Shoemaker, California
Nov. 6 1943

Dearest Kitty,
  I don't feel like writing letters but I guess I should write a few.
  Boy, I can say plenty but the language I would use wouldn't be nice. The sooner I leave here the better. I'm fed up already.
  I guess I can stand it for no longer than I'll be here. I'd like to see you, Kitty, but I'm afraid I'll be gone before I have the chance.
  By the way, I never received the letter explaining the one you and your girlfriend wrote.
  I saw your dad while I was home. I think you'll see him before long. He stays at Theo's. I was only home for 4 days but had a swell time.
  Well, kid, I guess there isn't any news so will close. You can write if you wish but I don't suppose I'll be here over 2 weeks.

Love
Bert

Nov. 10, 1943

Dearest Kitty,
  Say, honey, you took my letter I wrote the wrong way when I said you could write if you wished. I only thought I would be gone before I heard from you. I didn't mean it the way it sounded. I know it's hard to think of anything to write so write as you can.

Well, I still don't know how long I'll be here. I may leave any day.

You said you'd like swell to see me and wanted me to drop down over the weekend. I'd like to but they won't let us leave only 24 hours at a time every third day. I have tomorrow and Sunday to leave. I don't see why I couldn't come down because I don't do anything here but sleep, eat and see if I'm suppose to leave or not. Don't look for me but I'll try. No harm in seeing. My buddy and I were just talking. He has a wife in L.A. and he said he'd try with me.

Yes, I am in the same State as you and it is rather a disappointment, still it's better than where I was. The weather is swell anyway.

Oh, I wish I knew what they were going to do with me. This is heck to just lay around. I do know one thing. I'd have a better chance if I never had service school after my name. That's a mark against me now and I really never did anything wrong when I was in school.

Say, your dad told me when he came out if he had any gas left he might drive up here if I was still here, which isn't likely.

Hey, isn't Marilyn Hess in San Francisco someplace? [Editor's note: Marilyn Hess is the cousin of Kitty who later married John McKee. See Chapter 4.] *That's where I usually go to town. I spent a day and night there. It's a swell place for a sailor to get lost in.*

Well, I've run out of news. Oh, yes, I almost forgot. I spent an evening with Carolyn Killam the night of Halloween. We just walked around and talked over old times. She's really swell. [And one of my lifelong best friends.]

I heard, but of course it isn't confirmed yet, that us boys, I mean the ones that went through school with me, may have to send home our outfit and get different ones given to us. I hope it's true. I'll tell you if it's so.

I'll stop this time and write. Love Bert

Sun. Nov 14

Hi Kitty,

I guess it is I who owes the letter so here comes.

I don't feel much like writing. I guess I must be lazy. I'm plain disgusted at everything today. I want to leave and go somewhere but I just lay around and wonder. Oh, well, so much for weeping. I expect I'll get there soon enough.

Say, I got all the letters from Farragut. Even the one where you said you went with some little boy. Was he a sailor? I don't blame you, <u>kid</u>. I don't believe I should have written "kid." That use to make you mad.

Listen, Kitty, I'm telling you, never trust a sailor, even me. I think a lot of you but I've been going with other girls. I won't lie to you. I still think you're swell though. I'm just telling you I wouldn't lay around home and wait for no boy. Go out and have some fun.

You said in your last letter the only thing you like about California is the mountains and beach. I wish you could see the mountains in Idaho. They are simply beautiful. The only thing I like out here is the weather. I don't believe I could put up with a winter in Iowa.

I tried to get the 48 hours to come see you but never succeeded. My buddy did. He is in L.A. now but not me. I had to have a wife, sister or brother live there and I was afraid to tell a lie. I was afraid they would check up.

Has your dad come out yet? I expect you are getting homesick for him.

You haven't seen him for about 7 months, have you? You might not know him.

I have an uncle out here by San Francisco someplace. If I wasn't so lazy I would try and find him.

Gee, this place is getting empty. I expect I'll leave next week. Some of my buddies have left. Hope I get a break like they got.

Kitty, I've just got to clean up. I haven't shaved for a week. I haven't done nothing to be honest. I'll try and write more later.

Love (excuse this) Bert
I started to write your name.
Day dreaming I guess.

Nov. 15, 1943

Dearest Kitty,
Well this will be short and sweet because I'm plenty busy but I just have to write you a line.

I just got word I was leaving at once. I'll have my buddy mail this in the morn.

I expect there will be a good many times when you won't hear from me. Think nothing of it and keep the letters flying my way. I just won't be where I can write.

I went down to pick my liberty card up and they wouldn't give it to me. I guess they knew I was leaving.

Golly, I wish I could have seen you but it wasn't meant for us to see each other now anyway. If you are in California when I get back you will be the first one I'll see.

Well, this is very short but I'll write more next time. Don't forget to write. If you don't hear from me for a while remember you can always reach me by sending the mail to this address.

Love and Kisses
Bert
XXXXX

U.S.NAVY
Personnel Distribution Center
Pleasanton, California

Nov.16,1943

Dearest Sweetheart,

I was supposed to leave this morning but here I am so I'll answer the 2 swell letters I just got. I'm leaving at noon though.

So you still love your sailor. I can't say as I would blame you if you didn't. I've broken several promises that I've made, such as saying I would call you. I would now but I know you are in school. (Poor excuse isn't it?)

Why didn't you go out with the sailor? I want you to have fun. Just do me one favor don't get ideas about going out unless your mother says so. Gee! I hope you can go back to Iowa in the spring. I aim to go back there about then myself. I may be disappointed though.

So you finally heard from Carolyn. I guess you know without me telling you what I think of her. [I know you have a big crush on her, but sorry, honey, she doesn't feel the same about you.]

I guess it is plenty cold at home now. That's sure seems funny. To think now I won't see no more snow all winter.

Now I guess I won't even be around Thanksgiving. I thought surely I could get down there then. I sure wonder where I'll be. You know I had a cinch at this place. No work and 2 days out of 3 liberty. Of course I had to be back every morning. At first it was 1 day out of 3 and then my buddy started working at Battallion Headquarters.

I expect he'll be surprised when he comes back at noon and sees me still here. He went to San Francisco last night. A swell guy to be leaving. We wanted to stay together. I guess it's all for the best.

Well, honey, I must write to my Aunt so will close. Love, Bert

USO Nov. 20, 1943
Vallejo, Calif.

Dearest Kitty,

Well now for a short line after our short talk. When I called I was going to say so much and then forgot.

I'll try and put a letter by the censor. I have to go to school Monday and Tuesday. It's a gunner school. You see, I'm a gunner on a 20M.M., which is an anti-aircraft gun. I had better learn to shoot straight or maybe something might happen.

I'd sure love to see you now but it's almost impossible. I can't get away Thanksgiving I know. We'll have a lot of work to do. A lot of boys got 48 hour liberties this weekend but I couldn't because I have to leave tomorrow for that darn school.

Honey, I have something to tell you. You know I made a promise to a certain girl. I won't say what but if you really care for me I'll break that promise. You know I might as well tell the truth. I've went with several girls since we parted but really I still think of you. It's just that we are so far from one another and 8 months will change anyone, you know. I received a letter this morning from you. It sure cheered me up.

Well, thank Lord one swell guy I've been all through with is still with me. We have each other's address just in case.

Here's my address in case you have it wrong.

Love and Kisses
Bert

Elbert D. Judkins S2/C
"O" Division
U.S.S Stevens
C/O Fleet Postmaster
San Francisco, Calif.
11,27,43

Dearest Kitty,

I started to write you last night and was interrupted so I'll try again.

I received 3 letters from you yesterday. It was sure swell to hear from you but, hon, you do have the wrong idea about Carolyn and I. When I said she was swell I only meant as a pal.

Well, another day has ended so I'll finish this. I looked for a letter today but there was none.

I'm going ashore tonight for awhile.

Say, Thanksgiving I located my uncle out here. He's about 20 miles from me. I never got to see him only a short time but had a swell time.

Well, I'm afraid I won't see you but I will sometime, I'll bet.

I want you to forget about C.K. and me, it's only swell friendship.

Today sure didn't seem like Sunday. I've been working.

If you ever write to any of the kids back home you might send them my address. I haven't writte, but one letter home since I've been here. I got one today really giving me a cussing. It was sent to Shoemaker.

Well, so long, honey, and write.
Love,
Bert

Chapter 13

THE USS STEVENS
DESTROYER DD 479

The keel of the *USS Stevens*, a *Fletcher-class* destroyer, was laid down in Charleston Navy Yard, North Carolina, on December 30, 1941. It was christened and launched on June 24, 1942.

Of the 175 *Fletchers*, most were equipped with five five-inch gun mounts. However, it was planned that on six of them, in place of one of the gun mounts, a catapult to test the feasibility of launching an observation plane was to be mounted aft of the stacks. The catapult was actually installed on three of the ships, including the *USS Stevens*. Although not entirely unsuccessful, the tests demonstrated that aircraft on destroyers was at this time impractical, and the catapult was removed and replaced with a fifth five-inch gun mount in late-1943. But thanks to the semi-successful experiments with the *Fletchers*, years later destroyers would once again carry aircraft – helicopters.

The *Stevens* served in the Atlantic, escorting coastal convoys, until the spring of 1943, then passed through the Panama Canal in July. On July 28, it headed to Pearl Harbor, Hawaii, arriving there on August 9, 1943. It joined the battleships, the *Alabama* and the *South Dakota*, and escorted them, augmenting the Pacific Fleet. In late August, the *Stevens* and its task force and 15 carriers went to warm up raids on the Gilbert Islands, the Marcus Islands and Tarara Island. It then returned toward west coast of the USA.

In early December, 1943, Elbert D. Judkins, Seaman Second Class, boarded ship at Mare Island, San Francisco.

Invaluable to understanding the context in which Bert wrote the following letters is the history of the *USS Stevens* that my son, Richard, found (*War Diary: USS Stevens: 1941-1946* by Gary L. McIntosh, 2004, Trafford Publishing). Bert served on this ship for two years and two months in the Pacific Theater of World War II.

[LAST NIGHT ON SHORE]

USO

San Francisco, California Dec.   *5, 1943*

Dearest Kitty,

I expect you have moved by now but I must say that long goodbye. I'm leaving right away.

I'm writing everyone because I expect it will be some time before I can write another.

Sorry I won't get to see you, honey, but you know Uncle Sam, what he says goes.

I just got back yesterday from a short trip. I mean I really got seasick. So help me, I'll go over the side if it happens again. I saw boys lay down roll and scream and the worst of all is you can't eat even though they try to force it down you. Some are still weak.

Well, I had my picture taken and published today. Maybe you will see it. Do you suppose?

Tonight I'll admit I plan on celebrating. Really it's the first time for a month for as the Navy song goes, "To my last night on shore drink to the foam." That's what I and my buddy are planning to do.

Gee, "<u>kid</u>," I wish I could kiss you good-bye. Really, deep in my heart I hate to go but can't be a chicken. Write, sweetheart, and good-bye until we meet again. Love, Bert

It is early dawn and the busy Navy yard at Mare Island near San Francisco is covered with a heavy blanket of fog as the loud speakers scream, "All hands on deck, we are pulling out." The sailors tumble out of their small bunks, some with aching heads and puking bellies after their last night on shore. Confused and trembling with fear and anticipation for what is facing them, all hands rush topside as the ship begins to head toward the Golden Gate and the open waters ahead. Small tugboats, one on each side, are spouting plumes of spray upward as they gently nudge the bigger ship on. The tall buildings of the beautiful city stand quiet and sad on both sides of the bay. It appears to be sleeping as they leave her shores. Young men stand silently by the ship's rails and watch. Many try and hide the tears in their eyes, and their heavy hearts as they leave their families and friends and head out into the unknown. How many will return?

A hazy sunrise begins to appear behind them. It chases the fog away as the sight of the majestic Golden Gate Bridge looms ahead. They sail proudly under it. Some of the automobiles overhead honk their horns and the occupants wave from the windows as the ships head toward the open sea. With a final salute, the tugboats leave them and turn toward home. The *USS Stevens* continues westward. All of the young men on board watch the mainland slowly fade from sight.

According to Gary L. McIntosh, the *Stevens* arrived in Pearl Harbor on December 10, 1943. It remained in Hawaii until January 22, 1944, patrolling the islands, engaging in drills and target practice (*War Diary: USS Stevens*, p. 97).

Elbert D. Judkins S2/C
"O" Division
USS Stevens
C/O F.P.O.
San Francisco, Calif.
(Censored)
Dec. 10, 1943

Dearest Kitty,

Another day has ended so I had better write a few words.

I hope this letter finds everyone O.K. in California. I expect you have moved by now so will hope this is forwarded.

Has your dad arrived out there yet? Surely he has by this time. I'll bet you will sure be glad to see him. I guess it has been an awful long time since you saw him.

Well, there isn't much I can write about myself only I'm feeling swell. I could make a few complaints but I won't.

I'm anxious for morning to arrive so I can see if there's any mail. There should be some. There's nothing like a letter from home to chase the blues.

Kitty, I can't think of any more to say so will close. Tell everyone hi and write.

Love
Bert
Elbert D. Judkins S2/C

(Censored) Dec. 15, 1943

Dearest Kitty,

This will be short, no fooling, but if you care for me it won't matter how long it is.

You know I can't tell you much but I'm alive and feeling like a million dollar baby. Wish I were.

I haven't heard from you yet but maybe tomorrow. Boy! Oh boy! I had better or it will be too bad.

Has your dad got out there yet? I got a letter from Lina [Bert's oldest sister] *some time ago. She said he was there and told her to tell me you still loved me. Trying to keep up the morale. I guess that's all it takes, it's enough to keep me going.*

Gee! I'd love to get ashore here and go swimming. A good swim is just what I need. Some of the boys are swimming off the ship and I have to stand guard over them with a rifle and shoot any sharks that get too close.

Well, Kitty, I wouldn't even call this a note but I swear I'll write every day that I can get it mailed. Love and kisses, Bert

(Censored) Sun Dec.19, 1943

My One and Only,

Well, I finally received a most delightful letter. It's a good thing too or, oh boy, it would have been just too bad for a certain girl.

No, I wouldn't say a word because I know how hard it is for me to write even though I know I should. I don't write as many people as I used to either.

I think a lot of you, no fooling. I can see you as plain. I can turn back the pages and still see you walking down the street toward Theo's. You never knew how much time I used to spend looking toward your house hoping you would come down after a bottle of milk. I can confess these things now I'm a long way off. Remember the night you sat up because we had a quarrel? Well, I sat up too, looking for the little Ford to bring you home. If he had of!

I'll admit I went with a girl or two while I was going with you but if I had seen you with another guy! Oh! Well, that was different, it was me. Honey, no fooling I've been out with 3 girls in 9 months. One was in Montana, and the others were Francelia Nine and Leota Aldridge. One engaged Leota isn't for this sailor. So much for confessing. There isn't serious between any one of them. Please, don't be angry at me, will you?

I told my buddy today that if you weren't still mine after the war I was rejoining the Navy. I like the Navy life pretty fair now.

Say, I got a letter from Carolyn. Did she ever give me heck. She said she wanted my picture. I guess I'm really catching it now but what am I going to do? I don't have any more.

Well, I've not been ashore here so I can't tell you much about the city. In fact I'm about out of news.

Well, back to letter writing. I've been shooting the breeze with one of the fellows.

I got a letter from my sis yesterday, "Lina." She said she thought Fred was going across soon. He's still at San Diego. To heck with the Marines. I hate them. I shouldn't say that but I really don't care for them. I would give a lot to know the exact location of Homer but I don't. I expect he'll be going back to the states before long. Any guy that's been across has it coming to him.

I just happened to think you have moved now. Well, be sure and send me your address. Maybe this will never reach you. It better cause I've spent an hour trying to write it. Will you still go to the same school? I suppose so. So you want to go back to Indianola this spring. I can't say as I would blame you and if you want to I hope you do but leave those guys alone. Jealous aren't I? I don't care. I don't want every guy loving or pretending to love the girl I really love.

I expect your mom is plenty busy yet trying to find things she's misplaced. Boy I've helped move and I don't like it.

I haven't heard from George for a long time. He's really a swell guy. I wish he were here with me right beside me all along. I'm sure glad I'm in this division.

Well, Miss, don't break your neck to answer this but write as often as you can.

All the Love in the
World
Bert
Elbert D. Judkins S2/C

(Censored)

Dearest Kitty, Dec. 21, 1943
I guess I had better write a letter to the swellest girl in the world. Before I'm finished it will probably be a note.

I expect by now you are all settled down again. Well, tell me, how do you like your new home?

Gosh! Honey, you don't know how much I would give to spend tonight with you. Remember the night before I left for my training? I'll never forget those nights. They keep coming back and coming back. Honest, kid, right now if someone were to see me they would see a big tear running down my face. Oh! Why write all this? You probably say he's teasing me. There, I can truthfully say is no other and shall not be if I have my way. Even though you may not hear from me don't be mad, please.

How far are you from Bobby's? I don't suppose far enough but what you can still go there.

Tell Marilyn she's a good one. Here I was right in San Francisco but still I couldn't look her up, no address.

Just wait till I get back in the U.S. You will be the first person I'm going to see no matter where you live. That is if there isn't another guy snooping around.

I wish you could see my back. It's black from the sun. I guess maybe there isn't sun in L.A., is there?

Well, honey, I'm very sorry I haven't been able to send you a Christmas present but I hope I can bring you back a keepsake or two. I wish now you had all my Navy blues.

Well, sweetheart, be good and write. All the Love in the
World
Elbert D. Judkins S2/C

(Censored)

Dec. 24, 1943

Dearest Kitty,

No letter today and how I was looking forward to quite a number of them.

Well, it's the night before Christmas and what this little boy wouldn't give to be home right now. Remember a year ago? I sure do and I don't suppose I'll forget it. A certain sweetheart of mine was in bed. [I was in the hospital. I had just had an appendectomy.]

Well, it may not be so awful long before I'm home again, we will hope. Boy, I really want to see you. It's been an awful long time since I've seen you, almost 9 months.

I've received your letter saying you moved.

Gee! I sure hope you do get to go back to Iowa. I believe you will be more satisfied.

Now write and tell me how you enjoyed Christmas. I'll have a swell time, you can bet your life. I'm sorry I never got to send you anything but there is nothing around here. A few tokens But they are nothing. This is short but will let you know I'm thinking of you.

Love to the swellest girl,
Bert
Elbert D. Judkins S2/C

(Censored)

Dec. 26, 1943

My Dearest Sweetheart,

Here I am again trying to write a letter and I can't think of a word to say.

Well, how is my girlfriend? Oh! I would give the world to be with you, darling. If I could only see you, then you would believe how much I thought of you.

Remember the first night I kissed you? I guess if I hadn't of we might not think so much of one another, or do you? I can't blame you if you don't, I have been gone quite awhile but please give me one real chance to prove my love.

Oh! I'm having a hard time writing this. Suppose you had 4 boy friends looking over your shoulder. You better not have! Oh, one said to tell you he was a good guy. If you could have seen him tonight I doubt if you would have agreed. He got hold of some of that stuff you never wanted me to touch. He says tell you it's plenty good for you. Listen now, all this foolish stuff, don't get the idea I've been ashore. I haven't. I guess it is a good thing, he might have been a bad influence.

[Now the saga of Clifton begins. He and Bert were best buddies throughout the war. Both he and his girlfriend, Thelma, became pen pals of mine. Editor's note: Two Clifton Moores served aboard the *Stevens*. One was Clifton A. Moore, Chief Electricians Mate. The other was Clifton M. Moore, Gunners Mate 3/C. The latter was Bert's friend.]

"Hello, I'm the guy he's been talking about. All I had was a few beers and he thinks I'm drunk. Really I'm not. Anyway, a sailor's not any good if he doesn't get "stewed" once in awhile. That's what my brother thinks and he's been in this outfit for eighteen years. If a guy doesn't run around with other girls there's nothing left for him to do but drink and think of his girl back home. That's what I do, I think. You would rather have Jud drinking and thinking about you, than have him running around with anything with a skirt on, wouldn't you? Well I had better let Jud finish his letter to you. So long …"

Now, honey, don't let you get the idea I'm drinking because I'm not. I'm one that can still think of you and still not get drunk. I love you, darling, I can't think of nothing else but you. When I'm on watch at night and see that pretty moon it makes memories come back when I was with you. Gee! What swell times. They all come back in one wonderful picture. I can see you now sitting on those porch steps.

Well, my bud says he's leaving and to tell you good night, thank the Lord. He's silly but a real pal. He has a swell looking girl and thinks the world of her, too, but he is inclined to drink and to be

Honest, when I was in California I went out with him a time or two but here I don't drink. Things are too serious to be drinking, I believe.

Well, I hope you don't think this is too silly. Write, honey, please.
[I don't think it is silly, I love this letter.]

Love and Kisses, Bert
Elbert D. Judkins S2/C

(Censored)

Jan.1, 1944

Dearest Kathryn,

It's been quite a while since I've had a pen between my fingers so I'm going to write you a few lines.

I suppose you have gotten the letter I and my bud wrote. Well, we were just having our usual fun that eve. He had been ashore and just came back and had to tell me how things were, also what he done.

So you are counting on seeing me this summer. Well, here's hoping. I'm counting on it, too.

There's only one thing I like about it here, time flies fast. It seems like I was just home. I guess it's because we are so busy.

You don't like it so much where you are. Do you still go to the same school?

Say, I just happened to think. I won't need to worry if you go home now your old boyfriend is in the Army, so I hear. Your Norwalk [Iowa] *boyfriend, Onstot.*

Golly, I have a million people I should write. I got a letter from Marilyn. I was really surprised.

Well, honey, I can't think of a darn thing to say. I'll write more later, I promise.

Lots of love, Bert

Chapter 14

(Censored)

Jan. 1, 1944

Dearest Kitty,

And another letter I receive from you. How happy I am. I got quite a stack of letters today.

Golly, you sure make a guy feel good. I don't know what I would do if I couldn't look forward to seeing you. I hope you weren't kidding when you said you would be waiting. It won't be too long, I'm sure.

I sure get mad when I try to write and then can't say anything. It'd by far worse to write to the folks. I can talk of the many happy nights to you but them, they are full of many questions that cannot be answered and Homer, he's as bad almost. He thinks he'll run onto me but I doubt it.

Isn't Max Higbee in the Navy? If I remember, I believe someone said he was. Well, if he's got something like earth under him I'd love to have it beneath my feet. This water looks plenty deep to me. Oh, but life on ship is paradise compared to that hole in Idaho. I'll never forget those days. It wasn't the work as much as the school. I should put in my course for my next rate but that means brains and I just don't like to use what few I have, so guess I'll stay a seaman second class.

Say by the way, how many of my letters does your mom read? She may get kinda mad at me. We will hope not. It wouldn't stop me of still loving you anyway.

Tell everyone hi for me and tell them I can still picture those swell suppers we used to have. They certainly were the real stuff and not make believe like powdered milk. Why complain? It's eatable, anyway.

Well, I guess I've blowed long enough so bye now and write often.

> *Lots and Lots of Love*
> *Your true lover*
> *Bert*
> *Elbert D. Judkins S2/C*

(Censored)

Jan. 3, 1944

Hi Honey,

I never got the New Year started off so hot in letter writing but I'll try and make up for it in this letter.

What you all doing at home? I hope you are enjoying yourself but I'm also hoping that there aren't any boys stepping out with my sweetheart. As for me, well, I have plenty of little girls on the string. I mean mermaids, that's all it could be.

Today or maybe I should say this afternoon I have been looking through my letters of all the times you said "I love you." Well, I've begun to believe you do. I'm really sure.

Gee, I've got so many things planned to do after this thing is over, but who knows, I may serve a hitch in the Navy. I keep thinking quite a bit about it.

Say, you ought to see me now. I'll bet you will be mad. I have one of those things on my arm that you never wanted me to get. It's a rose. I have to remember these places someway.

We had to check our life jackets today. Mine wouldn't hold air. It was full of holes the rats had chewed.

This bud of mine is here again but he isn't bothering me for a change. Oh boy! We have some pretty good times, I and him, but nothing to be ashamed of, really. I see now he's writing to his girlfriend also.

I haven't heard from George or any of the others for a long time. I have never heard from my own brother in Indianola since I've left there but it isn't surprising. I know they aren't that busy so they just won't hear from me.

I hear from Homer's girlfriend lots. Maybe more than he but I'm very slow in answering her. I guess I just don't like to write very well.

Am I ever sleeping. I guess I'm either lazy or else its spring fever. It sure seems funny to see no snow and how I use to hate to wade it. I would almost give anything to be home. I guess this won't hurt me it's much better than Idaho anyway.

I hear another boyfriend of mine is in the Navy. If he gets the breaks I've had he won't mind it but if he don't, well, just poor him.

I don't suppose Bob has come out yet. I expect you will just have to go get him. I hope he does get to come out and I expect you are hoping too.

This I know is a very, very dull letter to read but I didn't want you to forget I'm thinking of you all the time. You are even my dream girl.

> *Bye Sweetheart*
> *And write Love*
> *Bert*
> *Elbert D. Judkins S2/C*

(Censored)

Jan 4, 1944

Dearest Darling,

It is growing dark outside and the show has started but little me has a sweetheart he is thinking about.

Honey, if you only knew how many times I think of you. I'm really lonely for you and blue but there you are and here I am. Why do we have to be so far apart and don't even get to see one another?

When I hit the states the first place I'm making for is wherever you are. I felt sure there would be some letters from you but no. I guess you do have a lot to keep you busy and then it takes so long for mail to reach me but I'll always be waiting for them.

I got a letter from Lina today. Her boy is leaving. It's plain down heck. I could say worse but won't. I expect he'll find the Marines are tough.

I saw in the county paper where Glen Hess was leaving for California. I thought he was out there.

Every time I think of the weather at home, memories come back. Good ones too and a few where we used to spat. I'll never forget the last time I saw you, quite a while ago, wasn't it? I hope it isn't that long again.

I guess I'm out of anything to say, so will have to stop. Remember, I'll be waiting for your letters.

> *Love*
> *Bert*
> *Elbert D. Judkins S2/C*

(Censored)

Jan. 6, 1944

Hi Honey,

I just tore up one letter I started but I'll try and finish this, then I must hop into my bed because I have to get out pretty early in the morn.

How's my sweetheart coming? Did you get over the flu OK? I hope you weren't very sick. I can sure remember once when you weren't feeling very well. I expect you can too.

Remember the little spats we used to have? Well, if I ever get in another spat with you, I want someone to kick me. Hon, I think you are the swellest person there is. I still have every picture you have given me and of course I have to look at them every day. My buddy tells me I'll have to bring you and come down to Texas and visit him and his girlfriend. They aim to get married as soon as he gets back. She's mighty cute, so is he. He lets me read all his letters. A trusty guy and a real pal.

Gee, come to think of it, I haven't heard from Carolyn for quite some time either, nor Barbara. Of course, it isn't unusual for George to be slow but he has other things on his mind. I wonder if he still plans to enlist. I'll bet he does a lot of swearing if he does. I mean I've done my share. I'll never forget that day. I was mighty proud. Well, I'm still proud but not so happy. It sure isn't what a dirty so and so told me it would be.

Say, do you ever hear from Velma Conklin? I just wonder if her and Kenny still get along. I won't forget what Kenneth told me once. I wish I were with him right now.

Well, Kitty, I'll stop this time but write maybe tomorrow.
Lots of Love, Bert
Tell everyone hi. Elbert D. Judkins S2/C

(Censored)

Jan 8, 1944

My Dearest,
Oh, these boys. To think I had one letter to you finished but tore it up. You see, I wrote on both sides of the paper and they called me stingy so I tore it up.

You see, this guy is here again. I wonder sometimes if you are my girl or his girl or a partnership. He writes about as much as I.

"So Jud is running me down is he? I'm the guy he just finished talking about. Don't let him kid you. He likes for me to write a few lines. He says he can't think of anything to say only that he loves you, but you know that already.

"Every once in awhile he reads one of my letters from my girl and does he get a bang out of it. I tried to get him to write to my girl but no can do. I don't see why he doesn't. He's one of my best buddies. Well, I guess you want to hear from him and not me so I will just fade out of the picture. So long, Clifton"

Back again. Say, I hear your dad is on his way out. I'll bet you will be very anxious to see him. I guess it's been quite a while since you have seen him.

Well, my buddy said to tell you he was going on liberty and wish I could come along. I expect it's a good thing I'm not, though, because he may come back like the last time. You should have gotten that letter by now.

Honey, I miss you so much. Honest, you can really trust me now. I wouldn't do anything that I know would hurt you.

Gee, us boys have some swell times together. Always kidding and joking each other.

I saw a swell show last night. Flight Lt. [Editor's note: *Flight Lieutenant* was a 1942 film starring Pat O'Brien, Glenn Ford and Evelyn Keyes. The plot revolved around a disgraced commercial pilot (O'Brien) who works to regain the respect of his son (Ford), against the backdrop of World War II.] *Every time I see a show I think of you.*

Honey, I expect you get tired of me rambling on and on so I'll close with much

Love
Bert
Elbert D. Judkins S2/C

(Censored)

Jan. 9, 1944

My Dearest Darling,

It hasn't been long since I wrote you but I'm always thinking of you so the best way is for me to express my thoughts in a letter.

I received three letters from you today and I was never happier in my life. I knew you hadn't forgotten me but I wanted a letter from you so bad. Now I really feel swell.

Well, sweet, I'm still counting the days when I get back to the states. I want to see you so badly.

This eve when I come walking in where my locker is, imagine what I saw. Well, that buddy of mine had your picture out and he was kissing it. I expect he saw me coming and thought he would have some fun. I mean to tell you that he makes sure that I don't go out with any other girls. It even makes him sore if I write to Carolyn or Barbara. He has to read them all before I send them, even yours.

I'll bet it is swell to have your dad there. Now I really hope you are satisfied and like it much better and listen now, you get busy and work harder in school, see? The boss is speaking, or is he boss?

Gee! Honey, I sure hope I can see you next summer. I'll really do my best to get to see the most wonderful girl there is. No kidding, honey, I know everything you say you mean. So do I.

Really, I could kick myself for a few minor things I have done. They didn't amount to much. As for the girls, well, I've only been with two since I saw you last. I don't even write them so you have no worry.

I'll admit I've taken a drink or two but I haven't been drunk or even silly. Most of the boys I'm with drink. Here I haven't even tasted it since I left. I've made some mistakes, a few that I can't correct, but here's one any man can correct.

I got a letter from my uncle today and he's about to go crazy because he hasn't heard from me. I know I've written him and I be darn if I'll write another. I don't like to write that well.

So you have been showing my picture. Well now, that's really O.K. What will I do if I walk down the streets of L.A. and someone yells "Hi Bert"? I've never seen them so don't blame me if they aren't good. One thing I am sorry of is that I had them taken with my flat hat, the white ones are by far the best. When I get back I'll give you about half the clothes I have. I never wear them.

Well, sweetheart, I'm getting short of breath so I guess I'll have to close this. I'll be thinking of you, dearest, so I want many letters. Be good, honey, and tell everyone hello.

> *True Love*
> *Bert*
> *Elbert D. Judkins S2/C*

(Censored)

Jan. 10, 1944

Dear Kitty,

This is the guy who is always bothering Jud. He told me if I started you a letter he would finish it. Jud went on liberty today and when he came back he sure had a big head, but he doesn't know what caused it. All kidding aside, Jud went ashore today, but he didn't get drunk.

Oh Yea! Jud and I broke out the pictures you sent him. He gave me one with you and your neighbor. It's really a nice picture. All I have to do is look at your picture and it will remind me of you and Jud also.

Well, I will close and let the one who loves you write you a few lines. So Long, Clifton

Hi Sweetheart, Now the main guy is writing. I should have finished this before now but was busy talking to the boys.

About the picture my buddy has of yours. Well, now I never gave it to him, he just took it and refuses to give it back. I wish you could meet him. He's really a swell guy. He's a third class gunner's mate and is my boss.

I got a letter from sis today, Winnie. You ought to write her.

She really thinks the world of you. She always talks about you. I guess she's not the only one that believes you are swell. I love you.

Say, I did go to shore today but there wasn't a thing to do but try to get away from an awful crowd.

Dearie, I wish I were there so bad, I'd never stop kissing you. I always have to kiss your picture every time I look at it and believe me, I get so blue that I can hardly stand to look at your picture. I love you, honey, and I'd do anything for you. I swear, no one will ever steal my girlfriend.

Well, I'll try again. I just tore up a page. It's almost bed time now and I'm really a sleepy person. I guess a letter to you is worth anything. I write you every day. Maybe you get tired of them.

Honey, I must close. You will always be on my mind. I love you, dear. I hope to hear from you very soon. With all the

Love in the World
Bert
Elbert D. Judkins S2/C

(Censored)

Jan. 14, 1944

My Dearest,
Here I am sitting and listening to the song "No Letter Today."
[Editor's note: This song was recorded by Ted Daffan's Texans in 1942.]
It is making me very blue indeed as we haven't gotten any mail on board for several days now and I'm one of the loneliest persons aboard.

Darling, now I'm listening to Bonnie Baker sing "Do I Worry."
[Editor's note: This song was recorded by Bonnie Baker and Orrin Tucker in 1941.] *Well, yes I do. I don't see why I should, as I know you aren't running around with other boys, but I just can't help it. If I didn't worry, well, I just wouldn't love you. I've always been jealous of you. I guess you already know that.*

Gosh! I have a whole page done. Pretty good for me. I hate to write letters worse and worse.

By the way, how long has it been since you heard from Neil? If you have his address, you could send it. These buddies will begin to think I've forgotten them, so maybe I should write him, as we used to be real pals.

I couldn't think of anything to say and my buddy just reminded me that he had a fight today. I never saw it but by the looks of the other guy we had better always be buddies.

I suppose Dick is really happy since his Dad came out. Does he still work in his spare time?

Well, it looks like we would have music again. Don't be surprised to see tear drops on this letter.

Honey, I can't think of any more to say so guess I'll just have to stop. Remember I love you.

All my love
Bert
Elbert D Judkins S2/C

Dear Kitty,

I hope you don't mind me dropping you a few lines once in a while when Jud is writing to you.

I just wanted you to know that I'm not a ruffian as he makes it sound like. I did have a fight today, but as I had a good reason for it, I know you won't think I'm a ruffian. Just think of what nobody likes to be called and you'll know why I hit the guy. Well, that's enough for that.

Here Elbert is sitting next to me writing your name all over himself. On his legs and everywhere.

I guess I will close for now. Jud is a mighty jealous fellow and he might think I'm trying to steal you away from him.

I just want to be a good friend. I hope you don't mind me wanting you for a friend.

Will shove off for now.

Clifton Moore GM3/C

(Censored) Jan.15, 1944
Clifton Moore G.M.3/C
USS Stevens
c/o P.M.
San Francisco, Calif.

Dear Kitty,

There Elbert is, sitting over there writing a letter to my girl. I haven't said anything to him yet about me writing to you. I'll tell him after I've mailed it. He's just sitting over there trying to make me jealous, which of course I am, even though he is my best buddy. I know he isn't interested in my girl. He only wants to be friends with her as I want to be with you.

I hope you don't mind me trying to make friends with you.

By the way, Kit, have you ever been to Texas? If not, you've been missing a lot of thrills. In the future (after the war), have Jud bring you down. It's really a nice place.

Iowa's alright. I've only been there a couple of times. Never did stop long enough to find out how friendly the people were. If they are all as friendly as Jud here, they're alright. He's a swell fellow. I'm not saying that because I owe him a dollar. He knows he won't get it back anyway. (ha ha).

Kit, there isn't much to write about. There's plenty to write about if only we could. I'll sign off for now. You don't have to answer this letter if you don't care to, but I'll be waiting for an answer in any case. So Long for now.

Your Friend,
Clifton
Moore C.M. G.M.3/C"

(Censored)
Jan. 15, 1944

My Dearest,

I just wrote you last night but I'll see if I can do any better tonight. A letter a day to the most wonderful girl there is isn't too many.

I believe my buddy is writing you again. I just finished writing his girlfriend. He's sure jealous and so am I.

Another boyfriend of mine has really gotten the blues. His girlfriend left him for another. Believe me, if mine ever does. Why even mention it? I have the most wonderful girl there is, so I need not worry.

Right now I have your large picture in front of me. The one of you alone, and you and Mary Jo in my hands. They sure make me homesick for you. To think I'm so darn far away from you. We will get together by and by. Believe me, it seems like years since I've seen you but those pleasant memories still linger in my heart.

I can see you when you used to get rather angry at me and I shall never forget the night I thought I heard the Ford in front of your place.

You can be honest with me now, how many times did you go with other boys after I met you? [So far I have not dated any other boys, not even the one from Norwalk you are so jealous of.]

As for me, I really never went with anyone else. Of course I sit with a few girls to see how much you really cared for me.

Well, honey, I guess I'll have to bring this to a close again. I could keep on forever talking about the things we use to do. The first time I saw you "at Neil's" I never supposed I could call you all mine, but I can, can't I? Your Darling, Elbert

(Censored) Jan. 17, 1944

Darling,

Am I sore! This is the fourth letter I've started to you. I never knew it was so hard to write. It's a good thing you are my sweet and not my folks or I'd say to heck with it and stop.

I did get a good many letters today. Three were from you. I'm sure glad your dad arrived when he did. How does he like California?

Jan. 18

Another day has gone by and as you can see I never got very far with my letters yesterday.

Well, I feel very blue today. Lina's boy, Fred, is over here somewhere very close. I'd like to see him but I don't know how to go about it. I don't know his exact location. She told me where he was and gave me his address. It would be much easier for him to come and see me if he knew I were here.

Say, you should feel pretty good. There so happens to be a very good show on and I'm writing to the swellest girl in the world.

Honey, there my buddy stands, bellowing, "Come on, fellows, the show is just starting." I can't think of a thing more to say, so guess I'll have to close. You know I love you anyway and maybe I can write tomorrow. Precious, take care of yourself and always remember I love you.

"Your sweet little sailor"
Bert

(Censored)

Jan. 21, 1944

Darling,

I expect I had better write you a line. I haven't made you mad, have I? Gee! Honey, it's been about three weeks since I've heard from you and I'm very anxious to know what's wrong.

I went ashore yesterday and looked over some more of town. It's really beautiful here. I wish you were here to see everything.

I hope you and school are coming along well. I sure wouldn't mind going back to those good school days myself. I had a lot of fun then.

If I don't hear from you today I believe I'll go crazy. I know you've written but I just haven't gotten them. I hope there are a hundred coming.

I'm sure in a fix today. My buddy ran off with my shirt and the rest are in the wash.

Well, I guess I've got to go to work. Honey, I haven't said a thing but I still love you. If you don't hear from me, remember I'm busy. I love you dear and always will. I'm just living for the day that I get home to see you. Tell all the folks I'm thinking of them and to take good care of themselves.

For always your
Darling Bert
Elbert D. Judkins S2/C

The *USS Stevens* missed out on the first hop of the leapfrog across the Central Pacific. However, she rejoined the Fifth Fleet in time to be part of the second jump. She was attached to Task Group (TG) 52.8, the fire support group, participating in the Operation Flintlock phase of the conquest of the Marshall Islands, in late January and February of 1944. She bombarded the islands before the landings and afterwards delivered interaction fire until it was no longer needed.

At this point in time, the war begins in earnest for our young Navy gunner. The sound of the ships bell rings loud and clear in the night, "General quarters, general quarters, now is the time for general quarters." The men run to their battle stations. The ship is dimly lit and the outside dark. The loud speaker tells where the attack is coming from and the men are told to keep their eyes open.

Bert runs to his gun and someone else goes to the ship's armory to bring shells.

(Censored)

Jan. 24, 1944

My Darling,

Say, I've been doing some thinking the last few days. Surely you haven't met someone else. The last letter I received from you was wrote Dec. 27. Oh, I may be just silly but I do worry. You still love me, don't you?

I received a letter from Carolyn. She never said much. She told me what was happening. The same old thing. But believe me, that old place will look plenty good.

Did my buddy write you? You know I went ashore and I'm afraid he said enough to make you sore. Listen, really, I haven't done a thing that would hurt you. I'll tell you just what I've done. I walked the streets mostly, then I had a large dinner and exactly 4 drinks, which were small. I swear I've reformed but will have to see if my will power is weak or strong.

Honey, I can't think of any more to say so guess I'll have to stop. I love you. I hope everyone is O.K. Tell them all hi.

Lots of Love
Bert
Elbert D. Judkins S2/C

(Censored)

Jan. 25, 1944

Dearest Kitty,

I wrote you last night but, honey, just to show you I'm always thinking of you, I'll write again. I've started two for home but tore them up. I can't think of anything to write.

I just read a letter that this crazy sap headed buddy of mine wrote to his future wife. The way it sounded, she is his wife.

Honey, aren't you going to write me? I want about a dozen letters from you. Please write them.

Sweet how is school coming? I hope you are better interested. You had better hurry up and get through. Are you going back to Iowa this summer?

Well, one thing sure, your old boyfriend isn't there. I'm glad of that.

Say, I guess my old loafing place isn't going be open any more from the way Carolyn wrote.

By the way, I finally broke down and wrote to Theo's. I don't know why, they haven't written me.

Well, honey, remember I will always love you, darling. Please take the best of care of yourself for me. You're mine, you know.

Your Darling
Bert
Elbert D. Judkins S2/C

Chapter 15

Early in the morning of February 1, 1944, the invasion of Kwajalein Island began. During this time, the *Stevens* made several sweeps up and down the beach, searching for targets. Late in the morning on February 2, Japanese artillery was seen firing on American troops. The ship unleashed six four-gun salvoes on the position. Just minutes later, no further Japanese activity was seen there. (*War Diary: USS Stevens*, p. 102.)

In the morning of February 3, the *Stevens* headed to tiny Ebeye Island, home of a Japanese seaplane base. At 7:32 a.m., the ship began firing on its assigned targets. With some short interruptions, the destroyer spent most of the morning and early afternoon firing on the island. Then, at 1:52 p.m., it began shelling a small piece of land just to the north of Ebeye, from which enemy fire had been coming. A mere thirteen minutes later, the *Stevens* returned to Ebeye to support the landings there. Although fighting on the island continued until February 7, the *Stevens* left the area on February 4. (*War Diary*, pp. 102-106.)

(Censored)

Sun. Feb 4

Darling Sweetheart,
I guess the time has come when I can write you a letter. Honey, don't blame me because I haven't wrote.
I've sure thought of you a lot. I hope everyone is swell at home. Gee, I'll be glad when I can hear from you. The last letter from you was written Dec. 25. It will still be the best when I can see you again.

It won't be long till spring back home, I guess. Wish I could be there. Believe me, time used to fly but I've seen it when it couldn't go by fast enough. The sooner this darn war is over the sooner I'll be home.

I've been worrying so about Lina's boy. [Bert's nephew.] *I wonder where he's at now. I'm really glad my mother is gone now. She'd go crazy.*

Darling, I've run out of anything to say but this will let you know I'm always thinking of you, dearest. I'll be seeing you again sometime. Don't forget to write. I'm always waiting for your letters.

> *All my Love to a Swell*
> *Girl*
> *Bert*
> *Elbert D. Judkins S2/C*

Upon leaving Ebeye, the *Stevens* headed to the Ellice Islands in the South Pacific. On February 8, the ship arrived at Funa Futi, Ellice Islands, where it stayed for five days, taking on supplies. The destroyer and its convoy then set a course for Koli Point, Guadalcanal, in the Solomon Islands. It arrived there on February 18, and the next day the *Stevens* left for Noumea, New Caledonia, arriving there on February 23. The *Stevens* would operate in this area for the next several months. (*War Diary*, p. 108.)

(Censored)

Feb. 9.

Dearest Kitty,
This certainly won't be very long but it will let you know I love you more than ever.

It's been so long since I've heard from you that I've begun to do a lot of wondering.

Gee! I wish I were there with you. I'd give the world to see you. It's been so long. It won't be very long till it will be a year. Just think, a year to be away from the swellest girl there is.

OH Boy! I just got two letters from you. They really make me feel good. One was written Jan. 12 and 13.

I guess you don't care for school out there, do you? You had better work hard even though you hate it and if you wish to go back to Iowa I hope you get to. I believe it's a pretty swell place after all.

So your mom thinks we really care for one another. You're darn right we do. I want you more than anything else. I sure wish I were there to enjoy the swims with you. We go swimming quite often.

Yes, honey, I'm swell. I couldn't feel much better. Except I'd love to be with you. So long, sweetheart, and write often.

Love Bert
Elbert D. Judkins S/2C

(Censored)

Feb. 11, 1944

Dearest Darling,

I received another swell letter from you today so I'll get busy and answer at once.

So you went to San Francisco. I sure like that. No, I'm glad you got to. I only wish I could have been there to see you.

Do you know what happened today? My pal took your letter and read it before I and then he gave it to me. It's a good thing he's a real pal.

You know, I really feel ashamed of myself. I've hardly written anyone. I've only written you and one letter home. Oh, I hate to write. I can never think of anything to say.

How did you find San Francisco? It wasn't much, was it, although it would look mighty nice now.

Do I remember all the basketball games we went to? I'd love to see another one but only with you. Honey, I've really missed you and it's a darn good thing I know you are waiting for your beloved.

I haven't heard from none of the kids at home. I suppose they are having lots of fun. I wonder what George can be doing. We used to have some good times together. I expect he will soon be enlisting in some branch of the service. Wish I could see him. I'd tell him to join the Navy.

I still haven't heard from my sister-in-law, Iris. I believe she's mad at me. Maybe she's busy but I doubt it. Not any busier than I!

Now look, it's 8:30 and I could be sleeping but no, I'm writing to the most wonderful girl in the world. I'm having a hard time, too. My pen seems to be scratching a good deal but I'm never too busy to write you.

I was standing watch the other day and thought I was seeing flying fish in the water. A warning came over the loudspeakers. It wasn't fish, it was snipers shooting at the ship.

Honey, I can't think of any more to write about. I really haven't said much now. Tell everyone hi and I sure hope you enjoyed your trip. I expect Marilyn is peeved at me. I've never answered her letter. Remember, dear, I love you so take care of yourself.

Your darling,
Bert
Elbert D. Judkins S2/C

(Censored)

Feb. 18, 1944

Darling,

I guess it's high time I'm writing to the swellest girl there is again. I won't be saying much but anyway it will let you know I'm always thinking of you.

Well, did you have a good time in Frisco? I expect there is always plenty to see and do. Gee, will I ever be happy when I can see you again. I hope it's soon but you had better help hope a little because it might be rather long.

Say, you are rather set on going back to Iowa this summer, aren't you? I hope you can even if it won't be for long but don't look at two many of those Iowa boys. They are sweet stuff, aren't they? Don't think much of myself do I? Oh, well, I got to say the good things nobody else does.

I sure don't know what's happening at home. I haven't heard from any of the sisters and of course not the brothers. Carolyn hasn't even written me for a long, long time. Here she is writing to you and not me. Can I make you jealous anymore? Believe me, I use to but I wouldn't even try anymore. I don't want you to ever be mad at me again. Should I say when I went home on leave.

Well, honey, I've been writing away and nearly filled two pages so I guess it's time to quit. Don't forget to write, honey, and never forget that I love you,

Love and Kisses
Bert
Elbert D. Judkins S2/C

(Censored)

Feb 24, 1944

Darling,

I'll attempt to answer the many swell letters I've received from you. I only got 6 from you today. It seems plenty good to get them, believe me. Now writing to my bud, well, I guess that's all right since I can always read them first.

Your mom sure wrote a swell letter. I'd love to answer but I'm so blame busy. Dearest, please don't think about sending me anything. I have plenty of everything.

[The next paragraph of his letter has been torn off. The censor does not like what he is writing to me. They have been in heavy warfare at this time. He says he is "blame busy."]

Gee, I wish I were there playing basketball with the boys. I haven't so much as seen a rubber ball. I'd sure love to get a little recreation of some sort besides laying around and just growing fat. Sometimes there's work but very seldom.

The way it sounds, Bobby may be leaving before long. I sure hope not. Really though, if he wasn't married it isn't so bad. Sometimes I think of switching over and serving a term and then again it would be rather nice to be home. I'll bet your little niece is sweet. She would have to be to be relation of yours.

Well, sweetheart, I must write to the folks so I'll have to stop. Keep those letters coming.

Loads of Love,
Bert
Elbert D. Judkins S2/C

(Censored)

Feb 26, 1944

Darling,

If at first you don't succeed, try, try again. Well, this is the third letter I've started to my darling this eve and I plan on finishing this. Tell me why when I start letter writing you are always the first on my list. Do you always think that much of me?

Say, I got a nice letter from George. I guess he's sure having the time of his life. Really, I have a great deal of fun myself but I'd sure love to share some with you.

I sure can't understand your folks but I believe they will be moving back to Iowa before long. Which do you wish for? I know which I would want.

I still haven't heard from Homer except that he's in the hospital and then the folks thought possibly he would be discharged. Here's hoping his health isn't that bad.

So you are wondering where I am. Well, I sure wish I could tell you but it's impossible, as you probably realize. [He is somewhere in the South Pacific. It is a mighty big ocean, and he is a long way from home. Editor's note: According to *War Diary*, page 110, he was in New Caledonia on the date this letter was written.]

I've been sitting here thinking what times we use to have and those wonderful dinners. Well, I couldn't exactly eat one now so shortly after supper, but I can sure think about them. They were really wonderful. Can you cook as good as your mother? [No.]

Say, Dick is making quite a sum of money to be going to school. Is he like all boys and always spends it or maybe I should say like me and always spends it? Oh, I'm saving a little but I do spend a considerable amount foolish.

I'm sure not getting along very good with my letter. The boys are raising Cain. They are all making so much noise I can't hear myself think.

You have been talking a great deal about Pat. Is she good looking? Maybe you should send me her address, what say?

I'd still like to know what you have to tell me. Nobody reads your letters only I expect for maybe a few exceptions.

Dearest, I've written for an hour and haven't said a thing, so I'd just as well close. I'll be thinking of you, dearest. Tell the folks hi! I sure hope your mom is taking good care of yourself for me. Write, sweet. All my love,

Bert
Elbert D. Judkins S2/C

Chapter 16

(Censored)

United States Navy
Feb. 29, 1944
(Mailed Mar. 2, 1944)

Darling,

I won't keep you wondering any longer, dearest. Believe me, I'm getting plenty of letters from you. Oh! I love to hear from you.

Say, I even talked about you in my sleep last night. Really bad, isn't it? I think of you all the time. I guess that should prove it.

Leap Year, isn't it? Golly, I never knew that till now. It doesn't look like any chance for me this year. I suppose I'll have to wait another 4 years, or will I?

Say, you mentioned about sending me a picture. I've never gotten it but I sure wish it would hurry. I'm anxious to see if you have changed any. I have a picture of you that I think is wonderful. I placed it in my bible. The two I carry over my heart. Remember the one taken under the rose tree? I think it's swell. I have all the pictures you sent me while I was in Idaho. I have to get them out almost every night and look them over. I expect your niece has changed considerably since the picture was taken.

When you asked me if I ever met Elizabeth Nisinger, I was almost afraid to answer it. You see, when I was home she wanted to go out with me, so I met her. Of course, don't misunderstand me. I never went with her. I really don't know her so terribly well.

I'm about to run out of anything to write about. You know, of course, how much I miss you, honey. I love you, dearest. I long so much to be with you and how I long for your kisses. Send me some, won't you? Write, honey. I love you. Be good and remember I'm always thinking of you.

> *Your Love,*
> *Bert*
> *Elbert D. Judkins S2/C*

(Censored)

March 2, 1944

Dearest Kathryn,

It seems like years since I've heard from you, darling, and it has only been a few days. You have really done wonderful in writing me.

Darling, I believe you when you say you love me. I love you also and want you more than anything else.

Remember the night I asked you to go to the show? I didn't know at first. I didn't know I liked you but was always afraid to ask you to go with me. Afraid the answer would be no or bashful, which? Well, anyway, you are mine now and for always till nothing ever comes between us. I love you, darling.

Wish I were in L.A. tonight. What a time we would have. You could show me everything. I'll be there someday.

I've sure caught heck since I was in Frisco. My pal says some guy you are for not dropping down to see you. I suppose I could have if I hadn't been broke all the time but when I went home it kinda cleaned my pockets.

Say, I'd sure love to hear from some of your new girlfriends. Maybe I could talk them out of a picture. I only want to see if they are as swell as some of the ones at home. Carolyn and Barbara, I mean. I thought they were wonderful.

I sat down last night and wrote George a letter. I expect he will be surprised to hear from me. A real pal he is but I'm afraid he's off on the wrong road. Dearest, I've changed a great deal but I know right from wrong.

You never liked for me to drink. I promised you once I wouldn't. I broke that promise, you already know, but since I've left I've never been drunk. Say, what am I doing? I may say something I shouldn't if I don't slow down.

Well, how's school? I'm glad to hear you like it better. Remember, you said you had plans. So do I, darling.

Well, my darling sweetheart, I guess I must bring this to a close. Don't forget to write. Why do I say that I know you won't. Tell the folks hi but don't let them read these letters.

All my love and Kisses, Bert

The *Stevens* left New Caledonia on February 28, 1944, and reached Guadalcanal on March 2. The next day, the ship made a quick trip to the harbor on Tulagi Island, then moved on to Port Purvis and fueled up. On March 5, it headed to Havannah Harbor on Efate, in the New Hebrides Islands. It spent ten days there.

(Censored)

March 5, 1944

Darling,

Believe me, I have a hard time writing to you. I can never think of anything to say and I know it must get tired reading the same old stuff.

I sure hope this finds you well and happy, dearest. You know I'm always thinking of you and your folks.

I had all my pictures out, admiring them. You know it's swell to be able to look at your picture even if I can't be with you.

Well, I guess I'll try and finish this horrible letter before retiring for a good night's rest.

I just saw a movie, "Youth on Parade." It wasn't so bad. It's been quite a while since I saw a good show. [Editor's note: *Youth on Parade* was a 1942 musical starring John Hubbard, Martha O'Driscoll and Richard Beavers. The plot revolves around a group of college kids who create a fictional perfect student. A psychology professor gets suspicious and demands to meet her, so the students hire a New York actress to portray her.]

Tell Dick it's a good thing he's not here hollering at me to turn out the lights when I'm writing you. Oh! I don't blame him. I like to sleep too.

I don't see how some of the boys here can find so much to write. It looks like it would be easy to write you but it really isn't. I know you get tired of receiving the same old stuff. I guess there isn't any more I can write about. I should have Clifton here to help me out.

Sweetheart, you know I love you. Boy, will I ever be happy when I can see you. You know, when I get home, the first place I'm going is to L.A., if you are still there, I mean.

Do you ever hear from Neil? I sure wish all the old gang were with me. We used to have some swell times together, Neil and I.

Well, sweet, I've run out of wind so that means closing time.

Please write whenever you aren't busy or so awful, awful sleepy.

I love you, dearie, and if I can't see you I want to hear from you. Say, you might let Tommy read this and then he could give me some pointers on writing to a real girlfriend.

Love and Kisses
Bert
Elbert D. Judkins S2/C

(Censored)

March 11, 1944

Darling,

No letter today but you have been doing wonderful. I've been receiving lots of mail from you. Just keep them coming.

I finally heard from my long lost brother, Homer. He talked as if he may get to go home. I sure hope so. [Homer is a navigator in the Air Force. He is serving in the Pacific on a bomber.]

Well honey as usual there isn't much to write about so this will be very dull. I'm listening to the boys talk about the times they have had, so there is a great deal of blowing taking place.

Sweetheart, I never got this finished yesterday but I'll try again this evening. Today I received the letter from you and Pat. The one with the fancy stationary.

Honey, you don't need to worry about those girls you were speaking about. I'm afraid you don't know where I am. I saw them, though.

Pat was speaking of Clifton. He's true blue so I doubt if there is much chance. A real pal if I ever saw one.

Speaking of that excessive drinking, dear, I only use it once in an awful long time and never excessive. Don't worry about that. Anyway, I never step out with anyone. Else. Sweetheart, I want you to love me always but I will always tell you the truth.

You were speaking of Pat having a very good boyfriend in San Francisco and the two were so nice since we are gone. I'll bet. Tell me who the lucky guy is.

Oh yes, I got a letter from my nephew. He tried to locate me but I had left. Now both are gone. He's sitting behind a typewriter. Lucky guy and I am glad of it.

Well, sweetheart, the movie will soon commence so good night and happy dreams.

As ever your Darling,
Elbert D. Judkins S2/C

On March 15, the *Stevens* left with Task Force 37 to attack Kavieng, New Ireland. The operation was an entirely Naval one without the landing of ground troops. It was successfully delivered on March 20, and the *Stevens* returned to Efate on March 25. Except for a brief trip to Espiritu Santo on April 2 and 3, the *Stevens* remained at Havannah Harbor until April 5.

(Censored)

March 23, 1944

Hi Sweet,

I'm mad. I had a letter to you all finished but now I have it no more. Clifton tore it up. He wanted to read it and I never wanted him to. He's standing over my shoulder now. If I say something bad, maybe he'll move.

He's left now!

Dearest, I sure have a time writing letters, even to you. I can never think of anything to say.

The last word I've gotten from you was when Pat and you wrote me. Now, how about her sending me a picture even if she does have another boyfriend? I want to see what she looks like. Is she a native of California?

Well, I have one whole page done and I haven't said a word.

I've finally gone back to using my brain again. I've been doing some studying for Seaman First Class. I guess I have to make it before I get a rate. It's very little I know about Seaman too.

Did you and Dick have to change schools? You will be going to school the majority of the spring, won't you? Tell Dick he'd better write me another letter and tell me all about L.A. I'm coming there someday if you are still there. I've heard a little about it but not a very good opinion. I'm sure it couldn't be so awful the way you write.

How about sending me Neil's address. I want to give him a piece of my mind. He's forgotten me, I guess, and I know he's had some time to write me.

Dearest, I must close this horrible letter. At least you know I'm always thinking of you.

All my Love
Bert
Elbert D. Judkins S2/C

On April 5, 1944, the *Stevens* and destroyer Squadron 25 left Havannah Harbor and sailed up the east coast of New Guinea. The destroyers reached Gili Gili, a former coconut plantation at the far north end of Milne Bay, on April 7.

(Censored)

April 6, 1944

Dearest Kathryn,
It's been quite a while since I've written you, hasn't it, darling? I hope you haven't missed my letters too much. I received two letters

from you a few days ago. They were the only letters I've gotten for a good long time. It sure was good to hear from you.

By the way, Clifton got a letter from you too. Say now, I don't like that he wouldn't even let me read it.

I hope you are all feeling swell. Gosh! I wish I could see you, honey. I really and truly miss you. If you only knew how much. I've not seen you for so long. I hope you are the same girl I left behind. I'll always love you if you are.

I'm afraid you will be right about the seven months. I'll likely be away longer, darling, but I know you will still be waiting. I love you, dearest, so you gotta wait.

Did you write Clifton's girlfriend? I wish you wouldn't. I don't believe she has the right opinion of me. Say, what about Pat, isn't she ever going to write me?

Golly I haven't heard a word from Homer for about two months. Can't understand why he doesn't answer my letters. You know he seems like a kid brother to me but I guess he isn't. [Bert is the kid brother.]

I guess Indianola is almost cleared of boys. You don't want to go back there, do you? I even believe Earl has gone. The majority are all becoming sailors. Remember what you told me once if I joined the Navy? I hope you have forgotten it.

Well, baby, I guess it's time I close this. I'm out of breath now. Goodbye, honey, and please write. I love you, you know.

As Always
Bert
Elbert D. Judkins S2/C

On April 19, 1944, the *Stevens* rendezvoused with others off Cape Cretin, on their way to the invasion of Hollandia. The *Stevens* reached Tanahmerah Bay on April 23, and began patrolling outside the bay. Very late the following night, the *Stevens* and others set a course for Cape Cretin. During the trip, seven crewmen were caught gambling. Six of them lost $18 of their pay per month for two months, while the seventh had his "rating" reduced. Apparently, Elbert was not one of these seven men.

On April 30, the *Stevens* and six other ships arrived at Humboldt Bay. The *Stevens* and three other destroyers then headed to Cape Sudest and Buna Bay, arriving there on May 2. The ship remained there until May 6.

(Censored)

April 25, 1944

Darling,
This must be about the fifth letter to you I've started and ended by tearing them up. This will likely be very short.

Golly dear, it's been a month or more since I've read a letter. Sure anxious to know how everyone is. Believe me, I really miss your letters. Of course, I miss you the most. I'd sure love to be with you. I'd take you in my arms and never stop kissing you.

This evening I'm sitting here almost asleep but am trying ever so hard to hold my eyes open long enough to finish this. If I don't send a letter once in awhile you will begin to think I don't love you anymore. I love you more than anything in the world.

Is Bobby still working in L.A.? I sure hope he hasn't been called into the service. Say, Mary Jo knows a good looking sailor when she sees one, doesn't she? I'll bet she is really sweet. Of course you think so. Tell all the folks hello. I'd sure love to see them all.

I haven't heard from any of the kids at home either. Oh well, no time is wasted in answering their letters. Phooey on them all.

Well, Clifton just stepped in of course he had to see who I was writing to. Do you hear from Thelma? I sure hope she has never said any thing to make you mad.

We had target practice the other day. A target was towed behind an airplane. I shot so many I got the order to "Stand down," and give the others a chance. It was just like shooting squirrels at home.

Well, darling, I must close this. Lights out at ten. Good night, honey, and write often.

Just Bert
Elbert D. Judkins S2/

Chapter 17

(Censored)

May 4, 1944

Darling,

Just a short note to let you know I still think of you, dearest. I expect you sometimes wonder since my letters are so few and far between.

Dearest, I love you but it is so hard for me to think of anything to write even to you.

I sure hope this finds all of you fine. I should write your mother but you can tell her hello for me. Sure would love to see everyone again soon.

I just had a little interruption. A very windy lad just entered. He's still blowing.

I heard from Carolyn K. last week. She never said much.

Do you still hear from Clifton's girlfriend? She wrote and said she bet you were really sweet. I don't bet, I know. Boy, Clifton sure gets peeved at me if I even write my own sister.

Well, honey, it's almost supper time. And I have a million things to do afterwards, so goodbye, dearest, and write often.

Love Always
Bert
Elbert D. Judkins S1/C

[He is now Seaman First Class, and he has not even mentioned it.]

(Censored)

May 5, 1944

Dearest Darling,

Golly, you have moved and I've been sending your mail to the same place. Oh well! Maybe you will get it.

I received your swell letter today. Sure was glad to hear from you, honey. Your letters are what keep me going.

How do you like your new home? It's about the same place you were, isn't it? Full of questions again, aren't I? That's about all I can do. I can't tell you anything.

It sure is a swell night. I believe I could fall to sleep now. Usually it's awfully warm and it takes hours to get to sleep.

Honey, I wonder about you so much. I wish I could see you if it were only for a short time. Of course, I miss you more than anyone else.

I guess this year has gone fast. I only wish they would move faster. I want to see you so bad.

How much longer until school is out? I suppose it's later than back home.

No, I still haven't received any word from Homer. Maybe he'll write someday.

Hope the folks are all fine. Tell them to drop me a line. Those letters are mighty scarce out here.

Well, honey, my eyes are about to close so I must stop.

Loads of Love
Bert
Elbert D. Judkins S1/C

[May 6, 1944, the *Stevens* retraced her steps down the east coast of New Guinea, then headed east to the Solomons, entering Purvis Bay on May 10. For almost a month she remained in the Solomons, escorting convoys, conducting combat training, and spending time in port.]

(Censored)

May 11, 1944

My Darling,
I'll try and answer some of the swell letters I've received from you.

So you have moved again. I'm glad you like your new home.

There is never anything new for me to write about, darling. I know the letters I write must be terribly dry but I try to do my best. Anyway you know I love you and that's the main thing.

I'm swell as usual. Still that same old person. Nothing will ever change me. I'm just a stupid little farmer that will never go back to the farm. I like this better than that.

Say, I wish you would destroy all those letters. Some of them are pretty rotten letters I wrote.

Come to think of it, just a month ago today you wrote this letter I'm answering. Kinda slow aren't I? It really isn't my fault, I just got it.

Sweet, I must close. I want to write Neil and then home, so good night, honey, and write often.

Love
Bert
Elbert D. Judkins S1/C

(Censored)

May 14, 1944

[Happy 21st birthday, sweetheart]

Hi Darling,
I hit the jackpot today. I received six letters from you. Swell! Gee, honey, I miss you and when I don't get those letters it's worse.

Please don't put any more ifs in your letters. You know I want you more than anything in the world. I'm just waiting for the day I can be with you and for always. We'll hope it isn't too far away.

When am I going to get those pictures? Very soon I hope. I want to see how much you have changed. Believe me, I've changed. I'm getting fatter and fatter.

I almost forgot I got a letter from George today. Kendall has been home. I'm sure glad of that. I guess he's Cpl now.

George talked as if he was going to try for the Merchant Marines. I've heard it was swell duty. I guess he's holding a pretty good job now.

Sure wish I could see your little niece. She has to be cute to be your relation. If you are always elected to take care of her I'll bet she's really spoiled. I wonder if she is spoiled worse than her aunt.

Well, sweetheart, this isn't very long but really I promise to do better next time. I'm very sleepy now. You will forgive me, won't you?

Love Always.
Bert
Elbert D. Judkins S1/C

(Censored)

May 18, 1944

My Darling,
Well, honey, here I am, not in person but in very fine spirit. Of course, I wish I were really the one being sent to your house instead of just a letter, but I guess I'll have to wait and be delivered later.

I received your swell letter yesterday. Golly, but I really love to hear from you. I miss you, honey, a whole, whole lot. You are the swellest girl there is. I haven't seen you for a long long time and still you haven't forgotten me. Some of these days I'll be walking in on you and I wish it would be soon but I guess I'll have to keep on wishing.

Honey, really I don't care if you write Clifton's girlfriend. I should write her myself but have been so blame busy. Gosh! I've got you to write and I imagine you think that is rather rare.

I saw a swell show tonight. Every time I go to a movie I think of you and the wonderful times we had together. I wish they would have never ended. I've always thought of you as the swellest girl there ever was. I really love you, dearest.

Say, I'm still waiting for the pictures you promised me and don't tell me they aren't good.

Boy, my sisters are sure hollering at me. They said the last letter they received was postmarked March 29. So you see I'm going to be busy tonight!

How's Mary Jo? Gee! I'd love to see her. I really love little kids. I hope she's over the chicken pox.

Gee! It's beautiful out tonight. Full moon, all I'm missing is a certain wonderful girl.

I expect it's time that I ring off and turn out the lights. Tell everyone I said hello. I sure hope everyone is swell. Goodnight, darling, and write often.

As Always
Bert

(Censored)

May 24, 1944

Darling,

I have a feeling this will end my letter writing for the evening. I usually start with you and end with you and call it quits.

Hope my honey is swell tonight? I do wish I were back there with you but I'll just have to wish.

I received two swell letters from you today. Gee but the fried chicken you were speaking of sounded good. Reminds me of some we used to have at home. I can never forget those days and nights. I had the best time of my life when I met you, although it never lasted long enough.

Sure hope you and Dick do get a trip back there. That would really be swell, honey. It's really a pretty swell place after all or maybe it's just some of the folks that live there.

I finally heard from Homer. He's been on another rest leave and finally found time to write me. I've just got to answer the letter at once.

I thought about your mother on Mothers Day. I went to church that day also. Oh, I get to church pretty often.

Darling, this is rather short isn't it? You will forgive me this Time, won't you? Be good honey and write often.

All my Love Bert

(Censored)

May 26, 1944

My Darling,

I'll start my letter writing with you. Gee, but I have lots of letters to answer tonight. I owe you more than one but I hope you settle for this one.

Honey, it's really swell to hear from you. I've read your letter about a dozen times today and of course I had to taste the lipstick.

I'm really glad to hear everyone is well at your place. I really thought if Bobby left you would keep the baby. I really hate to see him go but I guess it's a must. I hope he likes whatever branch he may choose and I wish him all the luck in the world.

I finally heard from my brother. It was about time, though. I sure wish I was as far along as he. He thinks he will be home soon and then I suppose I'll have a new sister-in-law. I hope she's somewhat better than one I can think of. I hardly ever hear from Theo's anymore.

Say, honey, aren't you going to get to go back to Iowa? Maybe you really don't want to. It would be swell though. I'd sure love to be there with you.

I was just thinking of how I used to manage always to meet you when you were coming home from school or roller skating. I remember when two girls were rather peeved at George and I. It is best not to remember those nights, isn't it?

What happened to you and Pat? I thought you were pretty good friends. Of course, it wasn't your fault that the two of you got angry.

Tonight is suppose to be a good movie showing. Won't you join me? Gee, sweetheart, I wish you could. It would be the most wonderful thing that ever happened to me if I could be with you now. I really love you, darling, and I miss you so much.

You know I have one favorite picture of yours. The one that was taken under the rose tree. I carry it in my Bible all the time. I really think it is swell. Sometimes I get rather homesick when I look at it.

Well, dearest, tonight I could write a book on how much I love you but I'd better stop and write to the folks or they will get peeved, I know.

All my love
Bert
Elbert D. Judkins S1/C

(Censored)

May 31, 1944

Darling,
Really, I don't know what I shall write about but I'll try to think of something.

This is a very dull day. Nothing to do but lay around and read or write letters. It's rather unusual for this to happen since there is so much to be done. I would rather be working.

I haven't heard from you for a good many days. I'm sure hoping a letter comes today.

Last night we had a band here. They were swell but of course my mind all drifted back to you. I really miss you, honey, with all my heart. After the band stopped playing we had two wonderful shows. One I had already seen and with you, too. I watched it all over again.

By the way, sweet, I finally received the pictures. Oh boy, they were wonderful but you had better keep me away from Los Angeles.

Have I ever been swamped with the Indianola papers. They all came in a pile. A lot of things in them rather disgusted me but I really catch up on the latest through them.

Is school out yet and what do you intend to do this summer? I sure wish I could help you spend a few days of your vacation but it looks rather dark right now.

For now I must stop but I will promise to finish later.

After about eight hours I'm back at it again. Boy, was I disappointed I never heard from you today. I know you have written and it just hasn't reached me but I just can't help but feel disappointed.

Suppose everyone at your house is O.K. I was sure glad to get the letter from your dad. These letters are really what counts.

Honey, this is ever so short as usual but when I hear from you I'll write a little longer one. Love always

Bert
Elbert D Judkins S1/c

[June 4, 1944, the *Stevens* sailed for the Marshall Islands.]

(Censored)

June 7, 1944

Dearest Darling,

As usual, this is the third time I've started a letter to you. I can never think of enough to say to finish it. It looks like this will be my first and last letter for tonight as I'm really very sleepy.

I was just thinking, a year ago I was home on leave. I sure wish I were in L.A. with you now. I want so much to see you, honey. I love you, darling, and gosh but I miss you. Every evening I lay awake thinking of no one but you. Really, don't you feel for me? I'm losing lots of sleep.

So your brother picked the Army. I can't exactly see why but surely he has a reason. Here's wishing him lots and lots of luck. So Ivan seems to like the Navy O.K.?

I believe I've already told you I received the pictures you sent me. Now believe me, you had better keep me away from Los Angeles. Are all the girls there that good looking? I'll still pick you, no one can ever change my mind. You are the most wonderful girl in the world, honey.

Well, dearest, I must bring this to a close. Tell your folks I said hello.

As ever, your beloved Boyfriend
Elbert D. Judkins S1/C

[June 8, 1944, the *Stevens* reached Kwajalein. The ship patrolled there until June 12, when it sailed for Eniwetok. It arrived at the lagoon on June 28, and stayed there until July 17, 1944.]

(Censored)

June 30, 1944

Dearest Kathryn,
It's swell to hear from you, darling. I really don't know how long this will be but it will let you know I still go on loving you. I'm dead tired from lack of sleep and then when a night comes I can sleep, I spend it writing letters.

I guess you have had some excitement back there. I'm afraid after one earthquake I would start back to Iowa. [Editor's note: On June 18, 1944, two small to moderate earthquakes struck the Los Angeles area, one at about 2:30 p.m. and another at about 10:30 p.m. Kathryn was in a movie theater when the latter quake hit. As for Elbert, in later years he experienced many earthquakes in California, including the 1971 Sylmar quake and the 1989 Loma Prieta quake (although he was well over a hundred miles away from the epicenter of this latter seismic event). He never considered moving back to Iowa after any of these temblors, having decided that Iowa's tornados are generally much more frightening than California's earthquakes.] *So you are going back. Well, honey, if you don't want to I'm really sorry you have to. I know there is lots more to do out there.*

By now you are likely vacationing. I sure hope you have a wonderful time.

I'm sure sorry to hear your mother has been sick. I hope by now she's well. These mothers, I sure feel sorry for them.

I sure had a laugh when you told me about Marilyn. That certainly sounds like her. I'll bet she's changed not that much, of course.

By now I expect Bobby has left and there are some broken hearts at your place. I know you all hate to see him go. That's only natural, but he'll be home maybe sooner than you think.

Honey, my eyes are closed now. See what I just done? I must write another letter home. So nite. Love Always, Bert

Elbert D. Judkins

Chapter 18

(Censored)

July 5, 1944

Dearest Kathryn,

I received two swell letters from you and your mother today. It was sure wonderful to hear from you but I'm really sorry to hear you were sick.

Honey, what makes you think I'm not thinking of you always? I'm so darn homesick to see you but what good is it doing me? I always think of you.

It sure is nice and cool this eve after the sun has practically baked me today but what I wouldn't give for some good Calif. sunshine.

Darling, I don't know whether I'm glad or not that you are going back to Iowa. It seems like you are getting farther away instead of closer to me.

Glad you like your work. Tell me what it's all about. What about school, did you fail in everything? You certainly hadn't better have.

Say, you and Vivian have been making plans that won't work with the plans I have made for you and I when you finish school.

I couldn't exactly make out what Mary Jo was telling me but I'm sure it was something good. I think you were very mean for not letting her write more.

Well, what did you do yesterday? Of course, you had to celebrate. Sure wish I had been there with you.

It's getting dark out here so it looks like I will have to close. I love you, darling, so please write whenever you can.

Love Always,
Bert
Elbert D. Judkins S1/C

(Censored)

July 9, 1944

Dearest Darling,

I don't know how far I'll get with this but I'm going to start you a letter. I'm way behind with letter writing but it looks like I'll get a breathing spell so maybe I can catch up.

I looked for a letter from you today but instead I received one from Barbara. She even sent me a picture. Now don't get no ideas, of course she won't compare with you but her picture was good.

Boy, I've sure been interrupted enough while trying to write this. My bud was sleeping here beside me and he just woke up and of course had to see who I was writing.

I got a swell letter from your mother. I sure think she's wonderful.

Guess you are happy now that school is out. Have you started working yet? Sure hope you like your new job and also I hope more so that you don't meet some Marine or even sailor. I'm still jealous as ever, the same little boy. Say, I remember you asked me how tall I really was. Gosh! I really don't know.

Honey, I can't think of a darn thing to write. Really there isn't anything I can tell you. I do love you, darling, and I want to see you more than anything else. Write me whenever you can because I really look forward to your lovely letters.

Your beloved sailor
Elbert D Judkins S1/c

(Censored)

7/12/44

Dearest Kitty,

I don't have a watch tonight so if I'm not interrupted too often maybe I will get a note written to you.

Darling, I received your two swell letters yesterday so naturally I'm feeling very good tonight. Gee! If it weren't for you I would never get a letter and occasionally I think you have met someone else. Guess you must love me a little or you would stop writing after not seeing me for so long. Now don't you dare let your work take all your time and stop writing. Bossy, aren't I?

Did I ever tell you I got the two pictures you sent me of you and Mary Jo and you by yourself? I thought the one of you and Mary Jo was swell but, well, I won't say anything about the other. Anyway, I knew it was you.

I'm really cooking right now. I hope it isn't this hot in L.A. I pity you if it is.

I just happened to think I owe your mother a letter. Oh, well! Maybe she will understand but don't you dare let her read this. Say, have you let her read any of them?

Honey, I would love to have the candy but it would be putting you to too much bother and then it does look rather foolish for me to be asking you to send me something. After all, I haven't gotten to send you a thing. I'll tell you what, just get in a package yourself and come out and see me. It's you that I want. I keep thinking about you and the swell times we use to have. I was really crazy about you and rather jealous at times.

What's everyone doing now? Suppose Richard is as mischievous as ever? Ask him if he still hides cigarettes out. What if your mother saw this? Wouldn't she be mad at me? I'm sore at him. I know darn well I've written him since he wrote. Hear he has a pretty good job. I hope he's a better saver than I.

I have two whole pages filled and still I haven't said much. How in the world did I ever do that?

I see I missed the show for tonight. It's a lot more important to write to you. You might get mad if I didn't and boy I wouldn't want that. I'd kinda hate for you to lose your temper. I have seen a little of it used occasionally.

Do you ever hear from Neil? Gosh! I've lost complete track of all my old buddies. He and I used to have some wonderful times together.

Sweet, don't be angry but I'm going to cut this short. I'm completely out of wind. I love you, honey, with all my heart and I will try and write again soon.

All my Love, Bert
Elbert D Judkins S/c

(Censored)

7/15/44

My Darling,

I'm warning you this will be just like all my letters, no news and very short. Oh, well! At least you will know I'm thinking of you.

Yes, and I do love you more than ever. Sometimes I get awfully discouraged because I can't be with you. I guess it's because I'm afraid you will forget me. I really miss you, honey. Sixteen months is an awfully long time to be away from the sweetest and swellest girl in the world. Believe me, it certainly can't be that much longer.

Maybe before awfully long you will be going back to Iowa. I'd give the world to be going back with you but if you are still in L.A. when I do get home I'll be right down to see you and how.

What a laugh. Now don't you dare write Thelma and tell her this but Clifton is copying the letter I just wrote you. He says, well, it comes from the bottom of my heart but I just can't think of what to say. It is terrible hard to write letters, the same old stuff happening day after day. I mean water and more water. I sound like I might be disgusted, don't I? I'm not. I just long for a certain little girl. She's cute, too. Remember how we used to stop under every street light?

Funny how those things all come back. Last night Clifton and I lost a lot of sleep just talking about you and Thelma. Everything we said was good, too. I've almost got him talked into moving to Iowa with me. I think it's a pretty swell place, how about you?

Say, honey, I never heard from you today. Maybe tomorrow. I hope I don't have to repeat that tomorrow now.

How's all the folks? Sure hope your mother is feeling O.K. again. By the way, is Ivan still around there? Tell him I wish I was on the same ship as he if he ever crosses the equator. That initiation you get there is plenty bad.

Well, honey, there's suppose to be a wonderful movie playing on here tonight so I'll have to say goodnight, sweetheart, and do remember, I love you with all my heart.

Love always
Bert
Elbert D. Judkins S1/C

(Censored)

7-16-1944

Kathryn Darling,

I just wrote you last night but to prove where my heart always is I'll drop you just a very short line tonight.

Now that I've started I can't think of a darn thing to say. Do you ever get tired having me repeat that? Oh, well! It's filling up space.

Saw a wonderful show again this evening. It's really about the only recreation we get outside of swimming and I don't care for that. Occasionally there is a beer party on the beach. So far I haven't been ashore. Of course, there isn't enough to get highly intoxicated on. Honey, really I don't care for it. I only told you this just to be writing about something, so don't get bright ideas please. I'd hate to have you mad at me again over nothing.

Do you still hear from Thelma once in awhile? She must be a wonderful girl from the way Clifton talks. Not as swell as my girlfriend, I know. No one can beat her. We sure have some arguments over you and her.

Gee! It's getting kinda late and I'm not done yet. I've been talking here with the boys, of course, about home. It looks like I've written a very short note, doesn't it? Darling, I just can't think of anymore to say. I love you, Kitty, more than anyone in the world. If

I could only see you. I really miss you, honey. I've got a question to ask you but not tonight. Now don't forget and write whenever you aren't too busy. Tell everyone hello for me.

All my Love, Elbert
Elbert D. Judkins S/c

[July 17, 1944, the *Stevens* departed Eniwetok Lagoon in the screen of TG 53.3 and transported troops to the Guam assault. The ship arrived the day of Guam landing, on July 21, and fired on enemy positions as troops landed. It left Guam on July 26.]

(Censored)

July 26, 1944

My Dearest Darling,

A nice cool evening. I believe the best way to spend it is to write to the most wonderful person in the whole world. Boy, that's really covering lots of territory, too, isn't it? I mean it, honey. I really love you, darling. Wish I were there just to spend an evening like we use to.

Clifton is sitting across from me and it looks like he too is having a hard time to think of anything to write Thelma. It's impossible to say what you would really like to.

It won't be much longer till you will be going back to Iowa. Well, I hope it isn't too long till I get back. Guess I could live another year out here if it's a have to case but I hope I don't have to. That would make it too long for us to be separated. You would likely have a husband and me, I couldn't even find a girlfriend. That just can't happen although I can't blame you for getting tired of waiting and just reading these horrible letters.

One whole page finished. Well, I may even get this done tonight before going on watch.

Remember how much coffee Theo use to drink? I'm just as bad now. I always drink three or four cups to stay awake while I'm on watch. It's a good thing we have it, too.

Honey, I sure hope your mother is well now. Maybe it will help her if she goes back to Iowa. And Dick, what does he do without those little Indianola girls he use to have. Maybe he's found one out there. Tell him I wish he would stay away from her long enough to write me at least a note. Got to keep on the good side of the relation. Tell me what I can do to gain lots of confidence from your dad and mother.

Say, sweet, you don't know how lucky you are to even get a two page letter, so don't be angry if I stop. I'm just out of wind and news so remember, darling, I love you truly and do write occasionally.

Love forever and ever, Bert
Elbert D. Judkins S1/C

[The *Stevens* returned to Eniwetok on July 30, 1944, then sailed for Guadalcanal the next day.]

(Censored)

Aug. 4, 1944

Dearest Kathryn,
Well, darling, I'm thinking of you tonight. Wish I were speaking with you in place of just writing.

I received three wonderful letters from you just recently. I guess they make me homesick in place of building me up. Why wouldn't they, coming from the most wonderful girl in the world?

I'm certainly glad you like your new job. Write and tell me just what you do.

[My job is in the big Methodist Hospital near downtown L. A. I love it. They call the young girls nurses aides, but mostly we do all of the dirty, cleanup work.]

So your mother is going back to Iowa. Well, what are you going to do? I think it would be swell if you got to go, too, and I hope you can finish school back there.

[I have mixed emotions. I love California, but I am homesick for the old hometown in Iowa as well.]

Before I forget it, tell your mother that Lina's boy was wounded at Saipan. I really don't know how badly as that is all she told me.

Bobby is in the army now. Well I certainly hope he likes it. Hope he can stay close by for at least a while.

This is sure a heck of a letter but can't help it. I promise to write again soon and I'll try to make it much longer. I have so many letters to write before retiring and I am sleepy.

Write lots, sweetheart. By the way, short letters don't make you sore do they? [No.] *They always do those sisters of mine.*

Love Always
Bert

[The *Stevens* reached Guadalcanal on August 5, 1944, then continued on to Espiritu Santo, arriving there the next day. The ship remained there until August 14.]

Elbert D. Judkins S1/C

(Censored)

Aug 7, 1944

Darling,

I'm a bit disappointed today. I never received a letter from you. I was really counting strong on it, too. It had better arrive tomorrow or I don't know what I'll do.

I've certainly been thinking about you lots, honey. I keep asking myself, now what can she be doing? Is she out with some handsome Marine tonight? I should know better than to think that. I want you to have lots of fun but just don't forget me.

I see my buddy has been on liberty today and it looks like he might be rather sick. I asked him what he had and he said ice cream. I can't believe that but maybe it's true. I don't know where he found anything to drink here.

Say what's this you say about you don't think drinking is so bad but you still don't approve of it. Honey, I don't want you to ever approve of it really.

I finally heard from Homer after about three months of waiting.

[His brother Homer was injured in a small plane crash on a mountainside on one of the Pacific Islands. Only he and the pilot were aboard. The pilot suffered a broken leg and Homer carried him away from the crash site for help. After they reached the medics it was discovered Homer had a broken back. What a hero he is.]

By the way, how is your brother doing? Hope he's coming along swell and I do hope he gets farther along than I have. Is he still near you?

Come to think of it, your mother is going to be leaving before long, isn't she? Well, now, do you intend on following her? I think it would be swell if you could. Guess I just don't like for you to be in Calif. Jealous maybe. I do want you all for myself. I love you, Kitty, honest I do. I'd do anything for you.

So, Dick is really growing up. I'll bet he has changed. Sure would like to see every one of you. You know I'm really fond of all your folks.

Suppose to be a swell movie on tonight. I very seldom attend them. Usually I write letters or go to bed. Mostly go to bed.

Sometime ago you mentioned getting a letter from Velma. Do she and Kendall still correspond? I wonder where Kendall is. Seems like someone said he was a corporal now.

It looks like I'm running low on words so I'm going to have to think of something to say fast.

Hey, how's the job? Like it any better? Don't work too hard I can just imagine you working too hard. Ha!

Sweetheart, I've just gotta stop. Sure wish I could see you but just remember I'm thinking of you all the time and I love you more than anyone in the world.

> *Your beloved Sweetheart*
> *Elbert D. Judkins S 1/C*

[The *Stevens* left Espiritu Santo on August 14, 1944, and moored in Purvis Bay on August 16. The next day, the ship sailed to New Guinea. It arrived in Humboldt Bay on August 21, and made a trip to Maffin Bay and back.]

TO: Miss Kathryn Kimzey
Indianola, Iowa

[I'm back in the old hometown and living with Bert's brother Theo and family for now. My family all moved home with Mother due to her illness.]

(Censored)

(Top of paper
torn, he says,
"Tearing, just
couldn't re-
copy it. Lazy
aren't I?")

August 22, 1944

My Dear Dear Darling,
A really and truly letter today and from you, too! Can't go around complaining now. It's really wonderful to hear from you again. I wasn't looking for a letter quite so soon.

Well, dear, I hope you are happy now. I wish I were there with you. I'd try to make you pleased. We did have some pretty good times before, you know.

That's right, this is a pretty season at home now but, oh, I can just imagine how cold it can get there. I do wish I was at least a bit cooler now. I'm practically cooked.

Was everyone glad to see you? I hope they aren't mean to you. If they are, just let me know.

Now you are thinking about school again. Won't be very long till it begins.

Say have you seen George? Sure wish he would drop me a line.

Maybe he's wishing the same thing about me. Try to talk him into writing if it's possible.

I'm getting nowhere fast with this and very soon I must go on watch. Better think of something fast or I won't have it in the mail tonight.

Gee, honey, I love you a lot. If it weren't for you I don't know what I'd do. I'd sure love to see you. Your pictures just don't keep me from getting homesick. They have to be real.

Well, darling, this certainly isn't very long but will let you know I love you more than ever. Write ever so often, dear.

Yours forever and
ever
Elbert
Elbert D. Judkins S1/C

Aug. 24, 1944

My Darling Kathryn,

No, I haven't forgotten you. I could never do that but if I don't hear from you in the near future I'll likely go nuts. I guess the boys can even tell when I don't hear from you. Now it couldn't be because I'm crabby.

Have you found a place to live yet? Now if I were at Theo's I wouldn't care if you never found a place to live. Certainly has been a long time since we were both there. I haven't forgotten those times, though.

Honey, can you find anything to do back there? I imagine there is a great difference between there and L.A. Soon school will commence, then there will be plenty to keep you busy. You had better work hard and get through school, too.

Has Tommy gone back yet or is he going? Full of questions aren't I?

Darling, I've just gotta close. Don't think because my letters are so short that I don't love you. I love you more than ever but still can't think of words to write even to you.

At last a letter and just when I was about to quit. Now maybe I can at least finish this page.

Oh! These girls, can Iris keep down her temper? I wouldn't blame her now as silly as the two of you must be.

Yes, maybe I've changed in a few minor ways, at least for the time being. One way is I have a very bad temper. I can still control it but, oh well, that's about all. One thing I'll set you straight on, there are no girls here and by the way I never have seen any south sea beauties or even ugly ones.

Kitty, why did you ever have to ask me the question you did? You know I love you with all my heart. Honest, I'm crazy about you. I'd love to live with you for the rest of our lives but you still have to finish school. Then if you still wish we'll get married, I promise. [My first marriage proposal!]

Well, sweetheart, I'll stop now. Remember, I'm always on pins and needles until I hear from you so write as often as you can.

Yours forever
Bert
Elbert D. Judkins S1/C

Chapter 19

September 7, 1944, the *Stevens* left Humboldt Bay for the port of Aitape. She joined Task Force 77 there, and headed for Morotai on September 10.

On September 15, assault troops stormed ashore at Morotai. The *Stevens* patrolled while the transports unloaded men and equipment. Late that afternoon, she sailed back toward Humboldt Bay, escorting the Australian ships HMAS Manoora and HMAS Kanimbla. The little convoy reached its destination on September 18.

The next day, the *Stevens* joined the McKee (DD-575) in the screen of another echelon bound for Morotai. The *Stevens* patrolled as radar and antisubmarine picket off Kaoe Bay and served on night patrol south of Morotai.

From September 23 to November 3, 1944, the *Stevens* remained in vicinity of Morotai. She continued her various patrols, fought off air attacks, and after October 25 served as headquarters for the landing craft control officer.

(Censored)

Sept 1, 1944

My Darling,
No letter today. I know you haven't forgotten me but do I ever get blue when I don't hear from you. Maybe since school has started it's taking up all your time.
Are you still staying at Theo's? If you see him ask him if he knows he has a brother out here. I would like to hear from him if he does.

I see I'm going to have to hurry this if I intend to see the movie. I'd sure enjoy these movies more if I were home with you. That's very odd, isn't it?

I got a letter from a buddy back there that said he saw where George Snodgrass was leaving for the Army soon. It doesn't seem like he's old enough but maybe he is. Well, the Army is O.k., I guess, but it's not for me. I'm all Navy. George should have gotten into the Merchant Marines. They are O.K.

Well, honey, has Indianola changed much? I never knew I loved a place so much till now. I guess it's really because you are there. I really miss you, Kitty. Sweetheart, I love you, if you only knew.

Remember how we use to spat occasionally? Gosh! And I'll never forget when you were in the hospital. I was sure worried. The first night I asked you for a date. OH!! Bashful me.

Clifton just left. He wanted to read this horrible thing but I refused. He's going to get married when he goes home. I wish we could but not till I'm out of here and for good. I read one of his letters Thelma wrote him. She's really cute. At least, her pictures are.

Well, dear, don't forget you have a fellow out here who thinks the world of you, so do write.

> *All my love*
> *Elbert*
> *Elbert D. Judkins S1/C*

(Censored)
Somewhere in the Pacific

Sept 8, 1944

My Darling Kathryn.

It's about time I answer your letter. I thought for a while I would never hear from you. I should have known you still cared for me but every day I see boys getting ditched, so I worry.

Honey, I certainly have missed your letters but not like I miss you. I practically cry myself to sleep every night. Well, maybe I don't do that but I would love to be with you and I am homesick, too. I guess when a person is in love it's only natural that he wants to be home with the most wonderful girl in the whole world.

Hey now, you just got back in Iowa and surely you aren't going to leave again. Can't see what people see in California but maybe if you didn't have to report to a ship or station it would be alright.

Right at the present I'm cooking from heat and to think back there it's fall, the leaves will soon be falling and it's cool. What I wouldn't give for Iowa. Say, you have started back to school, haven't you? Who is the boy that walks out of Stumps to meet you now? Don't take me to heart, I've got to have some way to fill the pages.

It's supper time and I've got to close. Movies after chow, you know. Clifton is here so it's a good time to stop. He's a pest.

Well, darling, I hope school doesn't take up all your time. I certainly look forward to your letters.

Love Always
Bert
Elbert D. Judkins S1/C

The terrible war rumbles and roars over most of the world. Our sailor is in the middle of the action in the Pacific. News is scarce in our little world in the Midwest. More commodities and clothing and gas and tires are rationed every day, it seems. Gold stars appear in more and more windows, Gold Stars that say, "Our loved one has paid the ultimate price for our country." When would it end? Many of our men meet monthly to discuss how to protect home and family in case of an enemy attack. They take turns at night patrolling the streets and neighborhoods, eyes glued to the empty sky, and ears alert to hear the possible sound of foreign planes flying over the quiet little town of 5,489 sleeping souls. Mother and the other women roll bandages and pack care boxes for our military men.

I am happy to be in school in the old hometown with lifelong friends. However, I miss the excitement and beauty of Los Angeles, California. My family and I are back into our old home on East Salem Street in Indianola, Iowa, just next door to Bert's old home.

(Censored)

Sept 27, 1944

My Darling,

Well another day has gone by and I'm still singing "No Letter Today." I can't complain though because you have been doing wonderful.

Gee! I never knew you were working at Burkeys. That's swell. I'm sure glad you like it O.K.

You aren't just kidding when you say you think it's about time I get to come home. I do too, but I have another think coming. I also think it will be quite some time before I do get home. Don't let that disappoint you. I want to see you awfully awfully bad, but we will just have to wait.

Say, is George still in Indianola? I saw where he had to register so I thought likely he had gone. Sure would love to get a line from him. Guess he is probably busy.

Say, honey, if you are still worrying about me and Leota just forget about her. She never writes me and neither do I to her. After all, I was only with her once and I don't think our friendship was much. So don't get mad and stop writing again. You know I was rather peeved myself.

Darling, you told me you didn't mind if my letters were short so guess I'll sign off. Tell everyone hello and write every time you aren't too busy. I love you, darling, and I think of you continually.

As ever
Elbert
Elbert D. Judkins S1/C

(Censored)

Oct.8, 1944

Dearest Kathryn,

For gosh sakes, please don't be angry because I haven't written, but honest, darling, I've started a dozen letters and every time something happens and I never get them finished. [Something like a war perhaps?] *I think of you just the same.*

Sure was wonderful to hear from you. Darling, you are the swellest person in the world. I know you are or you would completely forget me. If I get any mail at all there is always one in it from you and you can bet that's the first one I open.

Oh, yeah, the girls said they saw you. They keep a close eye on you, so watch out.

Well, how are school and you agreeing? I can just imagine. I could think of a million questions to ask you tonight but won't bore you with them.

Gee, I just wonder if everyone has the same trouble writing letters. If you could hear me curse. Oh, well, it's about time for the movie to commence and you know what that means.

Tell everyone I said hello. Heck of a letter but censors won't permit me to say as I wish so

All my love
Elbert
Elbert D. Judkins S1/C

The above is the only letter written in October, 1944.

On October 3, the *Stevens* departed Morotai in company with the Lang. The two destroyers put into Humboldt Bay two days later.

On October 16, the *Stevens* got underway in the screen of TG 78.6, Leyte Reinforcement Group One. On October 22, the convoy arrived in Leyte Gulf. The *Stevens* fueled before escorting TG 78.10 back to New Guinea. The Battle of Leyte Gulf was the largest naval battle in history. From October 28 to November 9, the destroyer accompanied three more convoys from the New Guinea area to Leyte Gulf.

(Censored)

Nov. 8, 1944

Dearest Darling,

Here's hoping you don't think I've forgotten you. Lord only knows I've certainly been thinking of you, honey. I received both of your letters and wanted to answer right back but, well, I didn't.

Hope everyone is swell back there. I can imagine that the ground is white. Could it be?

Oh, yeah, a good word from you and Theo broke down and wrote me a letter. What kind of English did you use on him? Well, did you get to see Homer? Maybe he never got back. If he never I certainly hate to live with him.

You said your Uncle Glen was coming back. Is he coming to stay?

Say, you and Beverly Nyswonger are getting rather thick from the way it sounds. Just what in the world do you find to do back there? It sounds as if Indianola is kinda dry.

Honey, time sure flies and I've got to go on watch so I'd better hurry this. Sure is short to even call a note. I promise to write a long one later so don't be disgusted.

Love and a
Great big Kiss
Bert
Elbert D. Judkins S1/C

(Censored)

Nov. 10, 1944

My Dearest Darling,

Just a hello before retiring for the night. Am I ever sleepy, too. If I were home now I'd sleep away about 10 years of my life. That is, I'd sleep at day anyway. You would probably keep me out most of the night.

Boy, it's a good thing I got these two letters from you. I had about given up all hopes. Well, I couldn't blame you. After all, two years and still no me is kinda a long time. It really means a lot to me for you to say you still love me. Well, honey, don't give up all hopes. I'll be back not later than two more years, I hope.

You said you would like to know where I was and what I was doing. I was at Leyte Island and I wouldn't know what I was doing. Maybe I was admiring the Philipine girls. They are cute but the wrong color. Well, now, they aren't much darker than I. I never got near them so don't worry, their big brothers were with them.

You said you and my nephew had been discussing my family. Now don't dig out many books, you might find out something you wouldn't care to know. I never traced my relatives back very far but believe me, I'm paying for something some of them, or me, has done.

Boy, oh boy, what's wrong with Indianola's football team this year? It sounds as if she's been taking a beating. Maybe their basketball team will be better and that sure brings back some wonderful memories. Have you forgotten them?

Sweetheart, I could rattle on and on but lights out, so goodnight darling. Tell the folks hello for me.

Love Always
Elbert
Elbert D. Judkins S1/C

It has been a month and a half since his last letter.
The war rages on and on, with no end in sight.

From December 9, 1944, to June 7, 1945, the *Stevens* operated primarily in the Philippines, the only break being a voyage from Lingayen to Manus. She then proceeded via Hollandia to Manus, then on to Leyte.

From December 20 to December 23, the *Stevens* escorted Ruticulus (AK-113) to Guiuan on Sumar and back to Leyte.

Between December 27, 1944, and January 1, 1945, while screening a resupply eschelon (TU-78.3.15) to Mindoro and back, the destroyer splashed three enemy planes during frequent air attacks.

(Censored)

Dec. 23, 1944

My Darling,

I imagine you have been wondering why I don't write. Well, dearest, I can't think of a single excuse at the present. Of course, just because I stopped writing doesn't mean I forgot you, not by any means. I've been thinking about you a great deal. I certainly wish I could be there Christmas with you. I hope you have a very merry one.

Now for a little news. At the present I'm in the Philippines. We were under an air attack the other day and shot down a good many Jap planes. Don't worry, we got them all, not a damn one returned home to tell their story. I guess this is about all I'm permitted to tell you.

A slight interruption caused me not to get this finished last night, so I'll try again. Has it snowed any there yet? It certainly is hot here but the nights are cool and that helps towards a good night of sleep.

I suppose you hear from Bobby quite often. Just what is his opinion of Army life by now? I can guess. Oh, well, we can always look forward to home and civilian life again and believe me that's something to look forward to.

Hope everyone back there is well. News from home is scarce. To be truthful, there just isn't any.

Honey, I know this is ever so short but I must eat supper so I'll say good night and I do hope I hear from you soon. Tell everyone hello.

Love Always
Elbert
Elbert D. Judkins S1/C

1944 is over and done. What a year it has been. Will
the war end soon? Will our heroes be home in 1945?
And they are heroes, each and every one of them.

A terrible storm at sea struck the area the *Stevens* was patrolling one night in December, 1944. The captain ordered most of the men below deck to ride out the severe winds and rain that rolled the ship from side to side. A handful of men remained on deck to keep watch. Bert shared the story of the storm with his sons many years later. He said the seas were so rough and the wind so strong he tied himself to his gun so he wouldn't be washed overboard. After the seas were relatively calm once more he was unable to get the water-soaked rope untied. None of his buddies noticed he had not returned below deck for a few hours. When they finally realized he was missing, they rushed top deck and saw a drenched sailor still tied to his gun. This was one of the few times he ever spoke of his career at sea.

Chapter 20

Now the *Stevens* operated primarily in the Philippines, the only break being a voyage from Lingayen to Manus. She then proceeded via Hollandia to Leyte, where she remained from February 13, 1945, to March 4, 1945.

On January 9, 1945, she got underway to escort a supply echelon to Lingayen Gulf. On the day before the convoy's arrival, it was attacked by six Japanese planes. Four were downed by the screen's antiaircraft fire and the other two fled. Bert told me later he shot down one of the planes.

On January 13, the *Steven's* convoy reached Lingayen and the destroyer patrolled on radar picket station. She stood by to deliver fire support if necessary until January 18. The *Stevens* returned to Leyte on January 23.

(Censored)

Jan 20, 1945

Darling,

Hi sweets. Gee! I hope you aren't sore at me for not writing. Dearest, the mail situation is very poor here. So far, I've been able to send but darn few letters out and none in return.

I'm still in the Philippines. We took part in the operations at Lingayen Gulf. I can remember back when I used to study about these islands but I never believed I'd ever see them. I know a place that would look lots better.

Is there still such a place as Indianola? If so, I bet it's dead as ___, well, you can guess.

Come to think of it, I haven't seen you for almost two years. You haven't changed your mind about me, have you? I certainly haven't changed mine. I still think you are the most wonderful person there is and I don't tell that to everyone. I know you have often heard a sailor has a girl in every port. It's impossible where I've been. It seems they are all Japs or maybe I should say were.

Honey, I'm sending a Philippine Peso in this letter. It isn't really anything but if I recall correctly you once mentioned me collecting various types of coins. I've been doing so but just never thought of sending them home through a letter.

Gee, I've slipped two pages almost complete. I've gotta quit. Do write to me, kid. It used to make you mad when I called you that, does it still?

Love always
Bert
Elbert d. Judkins S1/C

(Censored)

Jan 25, 1945

Dearest darling,

At last I heard from you after waiting for two long months. Nothing could be more wonderful, those months seemed like years.

Sure glad to hear Bobby got back to see you. He sure didn't get a very long furlough. Well, honey, I hate to see him go overseas but Uncle Sam's the boss.

I was certainly surprised to hear about Kendall getting married.

That gives me ideas but I guess it doesn't do any good. No one will have me.

And how I wish I were back there to take in a few of those basketball games, even if it is very cold. When they speak of snow I almost freeze.

Honey, I received your package. It was swell. I'm enjoying the pipe right now.

I hear Homer got home. I'll bet that seemed good after eighteen months out here.

Well, sweet, I have a good many letters to write so I've got to make them all short ones. I'm sure you can understand. Also, there's a movie showing tonight and of course I couldn't miss that. Do write every time you aren't awfully busy. You know I do love you and I love to hear from you, OFTEN. Love forever and ever, Bert

On February 2, the *Stevens* rendezvoused with TU 78.12.9 and escorted it back to San Pedro Bay on February 5. It then departed to rendezvous with TU 78.7.2 off Dulag. The Stevens guarded that convoy to Lingayen, arriving on February 9, and remained until February 13. It then returned to the Philippines from Manus and Hollandia, putting into Manila Bay on March 6. Also in February of 1945, the well-respected captain of the *Stevens*, W.M. Rakow, who had served on the ship since August of 1943, was replaced by G.W. Pressey, who in turn was replaced in June of 1945 by R.A. Schelling.

Pvt. R.J. Arnold 39594282   FREE
Cas. Co. 240, 74ᵗʰ Repl. Bn. (Sep)
APO 244, CO/ Postmaster
San Francisco, Calif.

TO:
Miss Katie Kimzey

Passed by US Army
Examiner 34291 Box 53-C

Indianola, Iowa

(Censored)

Mon. Feb 12, 1945

Dear Katie,
I rec'd your V mail written on Mary's birthday. I'm glad to hear you like to write themes as you'll probably have a lot of them.
As you know by now, I'm no longer in Hawaii. I could have sent you some picture folders but you know me. I didn't think they would

be too interesting. I'm now on one of the Marianas Islands. I can't tell you which one but I can say the climate here is very nice. We have a nice breeze coming in off the ocean so we keep pretty cool. The sun is pretty hot here and you can get sunburnt pretty easy. How well I know. There are lots of banana trees, palm trees, sugar cane and all kinds of tropical vegetation. As you probably know, there is no civilization on these islands to speak of. What is here has been built up by military personal. There are all kinds of frogs, toads, and lizards on the island. Big lizards, small lizards, lizards of all sizes it seems.

I went swimming yesterday and no matter where you might go in the states you could not find water so nice and blue and clean. Don't get the idea I like it here. I'm waiting for the day when I can walk on good old U.S.A. soil. I haven't been able to buy any film for the camera. So long for now, sis. Keep writing.

Love,
Bob

Brother Bob was in the infantry in the U.S. Army. He went through a living hell in the battle of Okinawa.

(Censored)

Feb. 20, 1945

Hi Honey,
Do these letters ever make me wish I were home with you. Gosh! It's wonderful to hear from you again. If it weren't for your letters, what would I do?

Things have certainly been happening back there. Everyone has surely been busy. What weather! Boy, it seems funny to hear you say it's been below zero. Of course, you wouldn't mind the snow.

Oh, yes, I received the pictures you sent me. I must say I have better pictures but they could have been worse. My sister keeps me well posted on you. She has really said some nice things about you. Of course, she doesn't have to tell me, I already know what I think. If a person is uncertain of love, this is one place he can soon decide.

Kathryn, darling, I wish it were possible for us to get married when I get back but it wouldn't be fair to you, not as long as I'm in the Navy. I know we could be happy and I do love you but I want to be with you. I've been thinking about this for a long time, darling, and it wasn't Jo Marie that gave me the idea.

Well, honey, it's getting a bit late for me to be up so I'd better hurry this up and get into my bed.

It was sure heck about Mrs. Hodson. She and Charlie were so swell.

Tell everyone I said hello and I'll try to get a few more letters written later. Remember I love you with all my heart.

Forever yours
Elbert
Elbert D. Judkins S1/C

On March 9, the *Stevens* headed for Lingayen, stopping over at Mindoro on March 10 and 11. The ship arrived at Lingayen on March 12.

From March 13 to March 15, she joined the Frazier (DD-607) in a search for downed American flyers. The Frazier picked up six men of a B-24 crew, and the *Stevens* was released to overtake and join TG 72.4 on the March 16. On that date, the *Stevens* fueled at Mangarin Bay, Mindoro, and then got underway with the Cleveland (CL-55), the Conway (DD-607), and the Eaton (DD-510) to support landings at Iloilo on Panay from March 18 to March 20.

On March 21, the *Stevens* arrived at Mindoro and immediately joined the screen of TG 74.2. The ship operated out of Subic Bay until April 14, 1945.

(Censored)

Mar.7.1945

Darling,

Hi, Honey, guess it's high time I drop the most wonderful girl in the world a short note. I'll say note because that is usually the way they end up.

Nothing new out here, just the same old story and believe me I'm waiting anxiously to return to Indianola to that sweet little girl of mine. You had better still be, anyway. I haven't received any mail from you recently so you see I do worry although I know that probably sounds silly to you but then two years is rather a long time and girls do change their minds. Of course, now boys never do, at least not me.

Have you heard from Bobby recently? If he ever writes and tells you which island he's on send me his address and also the names of the island and if it's ever possible I'll look him up. After all, if I can't see you it would help in seeing him. He's seen you since I and I could sit and just listen to him talk about you.

I got a feeling it's almost time for the movie to commence so I'd better hurry this up.

Listen, sweets, I'm waiting but not patiently for a nice big long letter from you and if you want to just crawl in a package yourself and come out with the letter, I'd much rather have you. You would love the Philippine Islands. I know probably better than I do.

Here I go on and on. Well, I am quitting this time. I'll be thinking a great deal about you, hon, and I'm sending you lots of

<u>LOVE</u>
Bert
Elbert D. Judkins S1/C

He's been away for over two years, and there is no end in sight for the war. I am enjoying my junior year in high school. Everyone worries about their loved ones overseas. When our beloved high school principal, Harry Grange, calls for an assembly the first thing in the morning, we all know he has sad news. I will always remember him standing sorrowfully on the stage, tears flowing down his cheeks, to announce another fallen hero. All of us grieve. Indianola is a small town and everyone feels like family.

(Censored)

Mar. 12, 1945

My Darling Kathryn,

It certainly seems like years since I have heard from you. I know I have plenty of letters out here someplace, or at least I had better because I'd certainly hate to be writing all these letters in vain.

Well, dearest, I hope you are in the very best of health and, gee, but I hope your folks aren't overworking you, if that's possible. Now don't take me seriously, I was only kidding. I've seen you work occasionally or have I?

Good movie tonight but it would be lots better if you were only going with me. Oh well, maybe it won't be too long until we can be together. I'm anxiously waiting for that day and I hope you are, too.

Gosh, it seems like I've almost run out of things to write about and only one page written. I'll bet these letters sound silly to you, don't they? Just isn't natural for a boy to be a letter writer. Honey, don't ever think because I don't write that I don't care for you. Honestly, I speak and also think of you everyday. You see, Clifton and I stand our watches together, which is eight hours out of twenty-four, so we are always talking about you and Thelma. It's the most wonderful way I can think of to pass away the night.

Say, you never mention Dick in your letters anymore. What the heck is he doing?

It looks as if this will have to end my letter writing. I'm out of paper. Of course, that makes me very sad since I love to write these blank things.

Have you ever heard anything from George? I sure pity the poor guy going into something he knows nothing about. The service may not hurt anyone but I can think of a place I would rather be.

Well, my dear, dear darling, interruptions so it's time to close. I'll be thinking of you and also I hope to hear from you and soon.

Your beloved
Sailor
Elbert D. Judkins S1/C

(Censored)

Mar 20, 1945

My Dearest Darling,
Well, sweets, here goes "the truth, the whole truth and nothing but the truth, so help me God."
Remember the letter you wrote in which you wanted me to do a bit of explaining in? Well, this is the answer. I'm sure I could do better if I were speaking in place of writing.
Honey, please forget about Leota and I. She doesn't mean even a little to me. I did write to her one letter in a year. I've written Barbara and you didn't mind. That letter didn't contain anything really. Just ignore her, or even let your temper get the best and tell her I said I never cared for her. If you wish I'll tell her in a letter myself but I think it best if I never write her again.
If you could have only seen me when I received this letter or better, I should say heard me. I did a bit of swearing and it's a good thing Leota wasn't around for me to lay a hand on.
[Many girls have a crush on my handsome sailor and they are trying to break us up so they can have him. Girls can be nasty! I am very jealous, but so is he. Considering where he is and what he is doing, I should not trouble him with things like this.]
Kitty, you gotta believe me, I love you, darling, and please never feel like are running competition. You are the only one I ever want. Let's forget everything, what say? I know it's hard for you to do but you will, won't you?
I'm really glad you wrote and told me all this and don't worry when I get home. I'll set a certain girl right.
Well, dearest, I'm running out of words so I'll have to close for now. Now do write and often. Next to having you your letters are the best. Give Mary Jo a great big kiss for me. After all, she's probably getting tired of kissing that horrible picture of mine and getting nothing in return.

The lights went out before I finished this last eve so I'll add a little. Guess there really isn't much more I can say, only I lost a lot of sleep last night lying in bed thinking about this letter. Do believe me when I say I love you. I couldn't ask for a sweller girl than you.

Love forever
and ever
Elbert
Elbert D. Judkins S1/C

[I do believe you, I am so happy with this letter I put lip stick kisses all over the envelope.]

(Censored)

Mar. 28, 1945

Hi Darling,

I'm warning you now, this won't be very long or newsy. Only a note but, sweet, my whole heart is in this letter tonight.

It has been several days since I've received any letters from you and believe me, I'm on edge waiting for the mail to arrive. Sure wish it would hurry.

Have you heard from Bobby lately? I don't suppose he could be located in the Philippines could he?

I suppose by now you have gotten your wish. At least it should be almost spring in good old Iowa. I can remember once when I wanted to leave that state but how I wish I could be there now only because someone very dear to me lives there.

Is Mary Jo still at your house? I'll bet she has grown a lot since these pictures were taken. I also imagine you have changed considerably. I hope not, I want you to be just as you were when I left, only of course you could do something about your temper.

[I was a little fifteen year old girl when you left home. I'm going to be eighteen years old soon. I have changed some, I have grown up!]

Well, darling, is there any news from back there? I'm certainly losing out. I've lost complete track of all the boys around there. Where the heck is George? I want to give him a piece of my mind.

Honey, I'm going to close this until I hear from you and maybe I'll have something to write about. I love you, darling, so do write and often.

Love forever
Bert
Elbert D. Judkins S1/C

Chapter 21

On April 12, 1945, our beloved president, Franklin Delano Roosevelt, died of a cerebral hemorrhage. Almost everyone mourned his death. Vice President Harry Truman ascended to the presidency.

On April 17, the *Stevens* entered Polloc Harbor and patrolled the area, screening the Denver. It delivered fire support until April 19, when it headed back to Subic Bay, arriving there on April 21 and staying a week and a day. On April 29, it returned to Mindanaro, stopping at Polloc Harbor and reaching Davas Gulf on May 1.

(Censored)

April 14, 1945

Hi Darling,

Am I ever having trouble just to get one letter written to you. The lights either go out or else I have a watch.

I've been hearing from you pretty regular now. A letter every day for the last three days and believe me, hon, there isn't anyone I would rather hear from.

Gee, I was kind of disappointed when you mentioned you might be moving back to California. Darling, if you do, you gotta go back to Iowa with me. Promise me, will you? I love you, honey. Please don't get too discouraged because I haven't shown up back there. I will someday, I know. Believe me, dearest, I think you are wonderful. Maybe you think I'm only giving you a line but by all means I'm not. I've loved you ever since I met you.

Now, you probably wonder why I ever had anything to do with Leota. Well, you know how Indianola is – kinda dead and I never knew exactly what I was doing. You told me once that you had forgiven me but I know how you feel. I want you to really forgive me and not just try to make me feel good.

I don't know what made me say that but darling I gotta know if you really care for me. I'd rather find out while I'm here than to come home and find you had someone you cared more for. Those things happen, you know.

Well, sweetheart, I'm almost out of ink so I'd better wind this horrible letter up. I certainly will be dreaming of you day and night. Remember, dearest, I'll always love you.

> *Yours forever*
> *and ever*
> *(if you want me)*
> *Elbert*
> *Elbert D. Judkins S1/C*

I feel he is getting more discouraged and depressed by the day. He later told me that at that point in time he was beginning to feel he would never be home. He is doubting my loyalty and affection for him as well. I admit I have dated some boys while he was gone. He told me to do so, but all of them know I am waiting for my sailor. There is one young man this summer I could take seriously. He is special. I agonize over, "Which one will it be, the sailor or Justin?" I chose the sailor.

(Censored)

April 23, 1945

My darling sweetheart,
I'm not full of much news tonight, dearest, but I will try to answer the two swell letters I received from you yesterday.

I certainly do wish I could make it home in June, darling, but no soap. You know I'm crazy to see you again but I guess Uncle Sam wasn't joking when he said, "We need men like you."

I wish I knew how Jimmy Lawyer got shore duty in San Francisco. Maybe he's acquainted with certain people that I never met. I wonder if you think as much of me as Ruthie does him? Would you come to San Francisco and stay while I was there?

Say, the way you write sometimes, things must not be too dead back there. I sometimes wonder a little. I guess you know I'm being a good boy and am not going ashore tonight. I can't trust my will power. They do have intoxicating beverages on the beach.

By the way, I got to visit the city of Manila sometime ago. There wasn't a great deal to see but it was rather interesting. It still isn't like the good old U.S.A.

Well, honey, this really can't be called a letter but I do think of you and I love you ever and ever so much. I'll try to write a long one in the future and here's hoping I receive another one soon.

Your beloved Sailor

Elbert D Judkins S1/C

(Censored)

April 28, 1945
Somewhere in
the Philippines

My Dearest Darling,
Noise, noise and more noise! Don't blame me if you can't read this. It's almost impossible for me to even think.

Honey, I received another of your swell letters today. I can't understand it but believe me, nothing could please me more.

You and Lorenelle are really thick, aren't you? Every time you write I believe you are together. Are you sure no boys are included in your parties? You don't have to answer that question.

Dearest, I'm afraid someone has started a rumor about me coming home. I only wish it were true. I will have eighteen months out here in June but I still haven't heard anything about seeing the states. Oh, well, the longer I'm out here the more money I can save and the more fun we can have when I get home. Now, that's looking at the bright side of life. There is a dark side and that's the worse. There are chances you might meet someone else. I don't know why I think of such things but I can't help it. I've seen a few of my buddies set aside and their girlfriends loved them, too.

Let's change the subject.

Good movie playing aboard tonight but Elbert has a watch. I probably wouldn't go anyway. I can't sit still that long. Now if I were attending it with a certain someone, it would be different.

It seems like my mind is on you more and more every day. That's all I think about anymore. I just wonder how much you have really changed. I know you have. I can tell by your letters. I love you though, darling, and I hope you think as much of me. That's what really matters.

Indianola must have come alive after the winter months. From the way you write, there is much more happening there.

Guess your brother has been having by far better luck with cards or such than I ever had. I've always been a loser until I learned to stop playing, or maybe I should say until we were told to quit gambling.

Sweetheart, I've almost run out of wind and you know what that means. I'll be thinking, praying and hoping that it won't be much longer until I can see you again. I love you more than anyone in the world, honey. Goodnight, dearest.

> *Love and many,*
> *many kisses,*
> *Bert*

On May 3, the *Stevens* supported minesweeping units in Santa Cruz area. It stayed a month in Manilla Bay and Subic Bay, engaging in exercises, upkeep and repairs.

May 5, operations in Europe ceased at 2301 hours (11:01 p.m.).

May 8, 1945: VE Day, Germany surrenders! The end is in sight! General Franz Bohme surrenders unconditionally.

> *Elbert D. Judkins S1/C*

(Censored)

> *May 6, 1945*

Dearest Kitty,
Seems rather strange that I haven't heard from you lately. It could be that you are very, very busy or maybe just tired of writing.

It does make one wonder after he's been receiving at least a letter every other day and then all at once they stop.

Darling, I've been admiring your pictures this eve. They sure make me wish I were home with you. Guess if it weren't for you I wouldn't have any reason to get as darn homesick. Seriously everyone, dear, there isn't a person I think more of.

I hope everyone is swell back there. I don't have to tell you how the news sounds. Good. Maybe it won't be much longer till we can be together and for good, too. It can't be too soon.

I can just imagine what things are like back there now. Nice and cool, birds singing and something to look at besides water and more water. Guess you can tell I'm ready to come home.

I just noticed the date and seventeen months ago I was leaving the U.S. bound for an unknown destination. Little did I know that I would see what I have without once returning.

Gee, hon, I've been rambling here for an hour and still haven't said a whole lot so suppose I just as well close until I hear from you. I do love you so write as often as possible. Remember, sweet, you are all the world to me. Bye now.

Forever love
Elbert
Elbert D. Judkins S1/C

(Censored)

May 20, 1945

My Dearest Darling,

Everything is peaceful near me for a change, so it's a very good time to get some letters in the mail, commencing with you, naturally. Why I should I don't know as I received a letter from a certain fellow and I hope he's telling tales out of school.

Kitty, if you have someone you like better back there, for gosh sakes, tell me. I can't blame you since we've seen so little of one another for such a long time, but I would like to know the truth.

There isn't anything new around here. I was on liberty yesterday and had my picture taken. I will enclose one in this letter if you want tear it up. I must say it's a good thing I got this news after liberty expired.

I'm not near Bobby. I'm still somewhere in the Philippines. From the sound of the news I'd better hang around here, too.

I suppose things were really popping around there when Germany surrendered. Sure wish I'd been home that day, wow!

[May 8, 1945: Church and school bells begin ringing all over town, the fire whistle blasts our ears along with police sirens. Everyone is running around the town square, yelling and screaming, "Its almost over, the terrible war is almost done. Germany surrendered today! Our boys will soon be coming home." This evening we built a huge bonfire on one corner of the town square, and a snake dance is beginning to wind its way in and out all around the town square. The festivities last all night.]

Darling, I've almost run out of things to say so I'll bring this to an end until I hear from you. I do love you, hon, and I'm hoping you still love me but if you don't mean it don't even write it in your letters. I hope this doesn't make you sore because I only want the truth.

I'll love you forever
and ever
Bert
Elbert D. Judkins S1/C

My Junior year in high school is finished. Mr. Grange, our principal, is going to work for the summer in the government ammunition plant in Ankeny, Iowa. He told my best friend, Lorenelle, and I that they were hiring high school kids to work there for three months. We applied and were hired, and began the highest paid and easiest job we would ever have. We ride the bus for 30 miles each way five days a week to Ankeny, about five miles north of Des Moines. We enter the heavily guarded gates and walk to our work stations inside one of the huge cavelike buildings. Lorenelle and I sit most days at a machine that makes gun belts out of live shells. Fourteen of them and then a red tipped tracer is fed into the machine. Sometimes we are assigned to a conveyor belt loaded with empty boxes and we fill them with the belts and shells of all sized. Often we slip a note to the military man who opens the box "over there." Sirens scream and smoke fills the air when an accidental explosion happened. Air raid drills are the usual thing every few days. It is an exciting job and we love it.

(Censored)

June 10, 1945

Dearest Kitty,

Well, Darling, at last I've found a few minutes in which I'll try to answer the three wonderful letters I recently received from you.

I knew you would be a trifle mad when you received my last letter. I had to know the truth and knew you would tell me. Honey, I think you are wonderful and I'm dying to get home so I can see you again. It's been so long.

I'm not doing too hot with this letter. I'm sitting here trying to think of something to write about and then all those old memories come back. They are all swell ones, though. I don't suppose I'll ever forget the night you and Barbara Jean got mad at George and I. Bet you could never guess what George and I did after that.

Gee! I sure wish I'd have had a bicycle the day you and Lorenelle were down by South River. Guess you two girls are together continually, aren't you? [Yes we are.]

Say, just who the heck is Keith Crawford you were speaking of? Guess I don't know him but from the sound of things we might just get acquainted!

Honey, I wouldn't ask you not to go out with anyone. It wouldn't be fair to you. You know what's best so let your conscience be your guide.

Lights are going out very shortly, so I've got to cut this. I love you, honey, so do write as often as possible. I promise I'll do better myself hereafter.

Love and more
love
Bert

On June 7, the *Stevens*, with TG-74.2, cleared the Philippines to support the invasion of Borneo. On June 9, the ship patrolled Brunei Bay. On June 11, the attack force went to Tawi, staying there June 12 and June 13.

The *Stevens* participated in the Balikpapan Operation between June 15 and July 12, 1945. On June 15, it supported minesweepers. Two days later, the destroyer bombarded beaches at Klandasen and fought off an air attack that evening and night. It engaged in shore bombardment on June 19. And on June 21 and June 23, the *Stevens* silenced two batteries.

Elbert d. Judkins S1/C

(Censored)

June 22, 1945

My Dear, Dearest, Darling,
  Time is short so this won't be very newsy. Just a line to tell you I still love you, honey.
  Gee! It was sure swell to hear from you. But you think I'm a good one after promising to write more often and then waiting so long before doing so.
  So Jimmy Lawyer got home. More power to him but I don't know how he does it. Guess all I can do is hope. I'm dying to see you, honest.
  Sorry, darling, that I didn't have some snapshots taken to send you. I did have the opportunity but neglected doing so. You see, it was the first time in eighteen months that I had been in a real liberty port, so naturally I had to look over the city.
  Say, not meaning any harm, but really I'm glad you can't locate a job in Des Moines. I'd rather you find one at home. I hope you do.
  Just what the heck are Theo's doing? Guess he's forgotten he has a brother out here. Anyway, among all the letters I received there are never any from him. Am I ever looking forward to some more of those chicken dinners we used to have, remember?

Well, darling, I've run low on things to say, so guess it's time to stop. I'll be thinking, dreaming and hoping that I get home (and soon) to see the most wonderful girl a person could ever want. Remember, I love you with all my heart.

Love and Kisses

Elbert D. Judkins S1/C

Chapter 22

July 1, troops land, and the *Stevens* covers them with harassing fire and counter battery. The next day, the destroyer leaves Balikpapan for Leyte Gulf. It arrives in San Pedro Bay on July 5 and stays a week.

On July 12, the *Stevens* leaves San Pedro Bay and reaches Subic Bay three days later. The ship conducts tactical and antisubmarine warfare exercises in Manilla Bay, Subic Bay area, for the duration of hostilities.

(Censored)

Philippines
July 18, 1945

Dearest Kathryn,

Hi, hon! Don't faint but it's really me. My word just isn't worth a hoot, I guess. I promise to write more often and what do I do? Write less. Too much liberty, maybe.

By the way, why don't you write me? Couldn't be someone else. Maybe Keith has added another lie to his list. Tell your dear little (only a good friend) that I'm gonna punch him in the nose when I get back. He'd better wish that I stay out here another twenty months. He sure told you a good one when he said he wrote to me because I don't know him from Adam. What the heck do you believe him for?

Well, darling, I hope you aren't working awfully hard. I guess you won't have much longer to work if the factory closes in August. I'm afraid your bullets are a little small in caliber for me to use but don't worry, you are doing someone some good.

Glad you heard from Bobby. He surely is busy or at least he'd write to his wife. Guess things have kind of cooled off up there now.

Honey, how's your morale? Suppose you never saw me for another year. Would you care for me any less? Things don't look so good but I can still hope. Guess I can stand it but it doesn't look like I'll be seeing you as soon as I expected.

By the way, I received the picture of you and Lorenelle. It was swell. Really made me wish I were home with you. I sure got a laugh out of Winnie. I think she thinks I'm raising h--- out here because she keeps telling me to be good. You are. Is that right?

Well, dearest, I'm going to close this. I've got to write sis. Here's hoping I hear from you and soon.

Love forever
And ever
Elbert
Elbert D. Judkins S1/2

(Censored)

July 29, 1945

Dearest Kitty,

I'm wondering if this will find you at home or in Coon Rapids. I hope at home. I'd hate for all this news to grow stale before it reaches you. Darling, do you get tired of doing all the writing? I think of you all the time but when I do have time to write it seems like I can never think of anything to say.

Well, as I just said, there isn't much to write about. Right now we boys are gathered back in our hangout, making a pot of coffee, and naturally there is plenty of breeze flying. I haven't been on the beach for quite awhile so there isn't any experience I can tell you.

Well, honey, I still am in doubt as to when I'll be seeing you. I hope it's soon as I am getting ever so anxious to see you.

Bet you could never guess who I heard from again today. It was Helen. That makes two within two weeks. They were only nice friendly letters so don't jump at conclusions. Besides, remember who gave her my address.

Say, I just happened to think this is Saturday night. I wonder what's happening back there. Bet the little town is kind of mild tonight. Wish I were there to speed things along.

Well, honey, I'm growing very sleepy, so will bring this to a quick close. Remember, darling, I'll always love you more than anyone else.

Love Always
Elbert

Elbert D. Judkins S1/C

August 15, 1945: VJ Day! Japan surrenders! The terrible war is over! Indianola and everyone here are wild again with the news. Bonfires and snake dances are all around the square until well after midnight.

Two weeks after the cessation of hostilities, the *Stevens* leaves Subic Bay with TG 71,7 and heads for the Yellow Sea and western Korea.

(Censored)

Aug. 20, 1945

Dearest Kitty,

Now, don't faint. I really intended to write before this but I could never think of anything to write about.

I hope this finds you O.K. I have received a great many letters from you since I last wrote. Boy, they all made me homesick, too. I've seen about all of the Pacific and her islands I care to see.

I can imagine what's been going on around there now that everything is over. It's a darn good thing I'm not where I can celebrate myself. I haven't been ashore for quite some time and that liberty wasn't worth a darn. Whiskey I never touch and women I never look at and that's all there is on this island.

Am I ever disgusted. I've got 21 months out here and under the present Navy Point System I've got three years to do before I get a discharge. I still have not the slightest idea when I'll be seeing you but I'm still hoping it won't be long. Gosh! I don't know how I've stood it this long. I really miss you, no foolin'.

Well, honey, this is kind of short but I've got to take a shower and retire for the eve. Remember, darling, I love you with all my heart and I hope to be seeing you in the near future.

Love Always
EJ

September 10, 1945, the *Stevens* arrived at Jinsen, Korea, for repairs. It then headed to Tsingtan China on September 19. There, it assisted in the internment of Japanese ships until September 29. The destroyer supported amphibious landings at Taku Bay until October 6. The next day, it left Chefoo Harbor and sailed back for Jinsen, where it stayed for five days.

On October 13, the *Stevens* left Jinsen with passengers, headed for the USA. It arrived in Guam on October 19, and Pearl Harbor on October 21. It made it to San Diego, California, on November 7, and arrived in San Pedro the next day, where it reported for reserve duty. Inactive overhaul of the *Stevens* began on November 19. The ship would eventually be sent to the Mothball Fleet in San Diego.

Elbert D. Judkins S1/C

NO CENSOR

Sept. 12, 1945
Korea

Darling,
Bet this will kind of surprise you to hear from me. I should have written before but there just never was anything to write about and then we went to sea for thirty days and just got into port yesterday. I don't imagine we would be in now but we needed repairs.

Guess everyone must have gone wild back there VJ-day, didn't they? I was at sea that day, too. What a life. We haven't been to a decent liberty port since we left the states. I did go ashore in Manilla a few times. I almost met my day there. I'll tell you about it someday, maybe. [He propositioned a young pretty girl there. Her brothers did not like that!]

Do you realize I haven't heard from you for a long time? Maybe you don't even care for me anymore. No matter what happens, I'll always love you. It's been so long since I've seen you but I couldn't ever forget you. Maybe I never showed it but I was always crazy about you and jealous as all heck. I've heard several things about you since I've been out here but it still doesn't change my mind about you. Some of the things you told yourself. I'm not in a position where I could object to them.

My buddy is leaving soon. He's getting a discharge.

Speaking of discharge, it looks like I will be a sailor for quite some time. It will only be in uniform and not in spirit. I don't get along with any of my petty officers. Guess that's why I'm not one myself. I only do enough work to keep from getting the officers on me. They are the ones who really count. Boy, we have some good ones. A new captain and if I would ever have to go into battle with him I would abandon ship first. I was under one air attack with him and that was enough. I still don't know how we made it. Luck, I guess. You know before I never could tell you what I thought of the Navy. Well, it's different now. I can and it's no good. [Editor's note: The captain mentioned above was R.A. Schelling, who served aboard the *Stevens* from June of 1945 to July of 1946.]

It sure seems odd to have all the lights on again. I like it much better this way. Just don't have as many worries. All you have to worry about now is running into a damn mine. I was sure scared coming here. I was below and someone hollers we are going through a minefield. I grabbed my life jacket and got topside and in a matter of seconds, too. It turned out they were spotting large jellyfish in the water. I saw them myself and I certainly thought they were mines.

Well, my darling, we are supposed to have a good movie tonight, so I'll make this short. I had to let you know I still loved you. I do, too, with all my heart. Guess you are awfully busy in school now so I won't expect too many letters but just don't forget me. I hope to be coming home soon but I have been disappointed before. In fact, we started back before but were called back out. We were bringing back a battle wagon for repairs. That was about 6 months ago.

I'll be thinking about you, honey. I think you are the most wonderful person there is. Again I say, I love you.

Love and lots of Kisses
E.J.
Sept 25, 1945
Tingtao, China

My Darling Kathryn,
Gosh! Hon, I feel like a heel because I haven't written more often but there has been too much happening around here for me to write many letters.

They are really keeping us busy here. We took over all the Jap naval vessels in this port so we have had a pretty big job guarding Japs, also trying to keep your own sailors from jumping ship and mixing with these Chinese girls. Last night while I had the duty, eleven sailors came past me and jumped back on ship. I didn't try to stop them and the officer of the guard caught them. I'm afraid I'm going to get a Court Martial out of the deal. I don't care much, just so it isn't a General, which might mean a dishonorable discharge and I don't want that.

Well, darling, from what I hear it will be some time yet before I will get to see you. Boy, I can hardly wait to get back. I don't know how I've stood it this long. I can't even look at your picture anymore, it makes me so homesick or maybe it's love sick. I'm not receiving mail here and that's worse.

Kathryn, very likely you think I'm feeding you a line when I say I love you. Probably you think I'm running around with girls in every port. Well, I'm not and only because of you but if I thought for one minute that you didn't like me I'd certainly start raising hell.

I know you have always objected to me for taking a drink and I don't blame you but being in the Navy it's hard to say no, especially when it's carried for that purpose and issued to each person individually when you go on liberty. You know I wouldn't have to tell you all this but I'm doing it because I really want you for all mine.

I suppose you are plenty busy since school has started. Your last year and then what are you intending to do? Darling, I've run out of news for now so I'll take a shower and write more later.

Back to this horrible letter. Bet this is really boring but it's the best I can do.

There's a group of Chinese on the fantail trying to sell some wristwatches. They are a cheap grade or I'd buy one. I've got to get something here if I can. They won't let us in the city. The Japs still control it and they are kind of trigger-happy. I'd like to make one liberty here just to celebrate a little.

Kitty, I'm going to close now and I'll try to write again soon. I'm really getting restless to hear from you. Seriously, I think you are wonderful.

Love Always
Elbert

[My Dear Jane letter. I don't understand why.]

Oct 1, 1945
Tientsen, China

Dear Kathryn,
Don't know exactly how to start this or what I want to say but here goes. Received a letter from you yesterday. Maybe I took it the wrong way but I feel things slipping between us.

Oh, well! I guess we were both awfully young to think of such things as <u>love.</u> *Maybe you were right when you hinted that you would have to get acquainted all over again. It has been quite awhile since we were together and we have both changed so much. Maybe you never meant anything but I just can't help but think that you are just not the same sweet girl I used to know.*

[I am the same except I've grown up. I'm not a little girl any longer. You have been through hell. I understand that.]

Kitty, it hurts like everything to say this but if we are going to break up I'd rather do it while I'm out here than when I get back. I could forget here but it would be much harder back there. No fooling, I used to worship you and I know no one could have cared for you more than I.

Gosh! Is it ever cold around here! Guess it will get me in shape when and if I do come home. I imagine it's getting chilly back there.

I sure hope you can go on to college. I have no plans myself and I'm afraid that now we won't have anything to talk over. You won't even have to write any letters since I'm the only guy you write to.

I sure feel like h--- today. My buddy, Clifton, is leaving today and we threw a party last night, him and I. Boy, if the old man could have seen us I'd probably be laying in the brig for a month or so. What a life. I don't give a darn for nothing anymore.

Well, kid, guess this is my last letter so here's hoping for a happy ending. I'll still think of you as a swell or the swellest girl I ever knew.

As ever,
Bert

[Goodbye Clifton. It has been great knowing you. We'll always miss you. Thank you for your friendship with my sailor. I wish all of the happiness in the world for you and Thelma. Good luck always. As for you, Elbert, I don't give up easily. We will have things to talk over when you get home.]

Chapter 23

The great war is over. Our heroes are coming home. People who left home as little more than children had survived homesickness and terror and witnessed unspeakable horrors. They returned as hardened adults.

Many would never return. Grieving families' and friends' lives were changed forever.

Our young sailor's brother, Homer, a Distinguished Flying Cross recipient, walked slowly down East Salem Street early one snowy winter day in November, wearing his medals and dragging his Air Force pack behind him. He went past our home at 808 East Salem and surprised his brother and family at their home on down the street. What a happy reunion it was.

But where is my sailor? The one who broke my heart a few weeks ago. The one who thought he would never be home again.

November in Iowa is usually a dreary month. But not this year. Thanksgiving is on its way and it is a festive time, especially this year since the terrible war is done.

It is beginning to snow in the early afternoon of November 8, 1945. It has been over a month since I got my last letter from Bert. School is out for the day and I hurry home and walk up the steps to my front door. My mother opens the door. She says, "Bert just got home, he stopped here to say hello to me then he went to his brother's home. He isn't the same boy who left here so long ago. He is quiet, and thin, and …"

I don't wait to hear any more. I drop my school books and run back down the five porch steps and I don't stop until I reach the Judkinses' home.

We never knock before entering our dear friends' home. I open their door and burst into the living room, straight into the open arms of my beloved sailor. Tears glisten in his big brown eyes and my tears flow down my cheeks onto the front of his Navy Blue uniform. I want to hold him forever. I don't ever want to let him go.

He is home after almost three years living on a Navy destroyer halfway around the world. The harsh words in his last letter to me are forgotten. We are together again. It is a joyous time we will always remember.

My senior class in the local high school is almost forgotten for now. Bert insists I must attend, but my heart is with him. I am so proud of the handsome young man in uniform who waits daily outside the high school at 3 p.m. for me to rush into his waiting arms. He is learning to smile again. Many young men who have lived through the horrors of war are returning home, and being welcomed by family and friends.

Bert and I spend all of our leisure hours together. We talk, and visit family and friends, and make plans for our life together.

The cold snowy winter days are filled with our love and joy. We attend movies and ball games. A special treat is sledding parties at Devils Elbow Hill under a full winter moon. A large bonfire burns at the top of the hill. Screams of laughter echo from those trying to negotiate the sharp turns at the bottom of the crooked hill while riding on their sleds at top speed. The fragrance of roasting marshmallows and hot dogs fill the air just like before the terrible war stole these things away. Young friends gather together, mothers prepare the returning veterans' favorite meals. "We need to fatten the boys up. They are too skinny," my mother says. She cooks a lot of fried chicken and mashed potatoes and gravy and apple pie for our boys. Aunt Susie finally opens the large can of Van Camps Pork and Beans she had been saving for Bert's return. They were a special treat for him.

We spend many hours with Bert's large family. I am beginning to love them like I love my own.

We laugh because many of Bert's old girlfriends continue to try to steal him away from me. They phone and invite him out. Sometimes he says, "Sure, I'll meet you." He then takes me with him. The girls look so disappointed when they see him standing there and holding my hand.

A favorite gentleman friend of ours, Grandpa Hodson, loans us his old car to drive while he is home on leave. The town marshal laughs and tells Bert he really should get a driver's license soon. That was a small detail Bert had neglected to do for years.

We travel the countryside over frozen roads to see all of the folks and things he has missed in the past three years.

I want to go back to California with him when his leave is over. He wants me to finish my senior year in school first. We will be married late next spring when his Navy career is over.

One afternoon near Thanksgiving Bert and his brother, Homer, tell me they have some errands to do in Des Moines. They will meet me in Lucas Café, the local hangout for kids, after the high school football game that night. They smile at each other and seem a little mysterious about their errand in the big city.

After the game is over I sit in the front booth in the café with some friends and wait for the front door to open. One of the most persistent, hopeful girls for Bert's affections, Leota, sits in the booth behind us. Suddenly the front door opens and Bert and Homer, both in uniform, walk in. I hurry to meet them. How proud I am having two handsome military men waiting for me.

The sailor takes a small velvet box out of his peacoat pocket and opens it. In front of all of the town kids he looks into my eyes and says, "I love you, Kitty, will you marry me?" He places a large diamond ring on my third finger left hand. The people in the café erupt into cheers. After I say, "Yes," and kiss my fiance and give Homer a hug, I turn and walk to the booth where Leota is sitting with an astonished look on her face. I hold my left hand with the beautiful diamond ring on my finger in front of her face. "See the ring, Leota? He's all mine now." She and her friends left the café.

Bert later told me he didn't have quite enough money to buy the ring he wanted, so Homer pitched in and helped him pay for it. It became a lifelong joke between us: Which one was I really engaged to?

All too soon our glorious November is coming to an end. My beloved sailor has to prepare for the end of his leave. He will report to San Pedro, California, and once again board the *USS Stevens*. The men are going to begin "inactive overhaul" on the majestic ship and prepare her to eventually join the Mothball Fleet in San Diego, California. She is only five years old. She and her courageous crew fought a grand fight. She deserves a long rest now.

[Editor's note: Just months after Kitty's death in February of 2012, the home of one of her children was burglarized. Sadly, one of the items that was stolen was the diamond ring she wore for more than sixty-six years of her life.]

December 7, 1945

Once again an icy wind is blowing around the corners and down the deserted streets of Des Moines, Iowa. Our small group, my mother, Bert's brother, Theo, and sister-in-law, Iris, and I are clustered around our blue clad sailor on the platform of the Rock Island train station. The cry of a whistle echo's through the night. We are not as fearful as we were three years ago when we watched the ominous approach of a troop train roar down the tracks toward us. The war is over, and our loved one will soon be home forever. The train screeches to a stop and the door is opened. A smiling porter waits as we all kiss our man goodbye.

"Write often, you will be home soon, we love you," we call as the door closes behind him.

The train chugs into the darkness with the mournful whistle wailing. How different this parting is from the last one. This is only temporary. He will be safely home in the spring.

I am writing nightly letters once again. I am waiting daily for the mailman to bring me a letter that begins, "Dearest Kitty".

Chapter 24

The following are excerpts from Bert's letters to 2-10-1946.

Elbert D. Judkins S1/C USS Stevens
FPO San Francisco, CA.
Dec. 10, 1945

Dearest Kitty,

Well, darling, made it back but wish to h--- I was home with you. I didn't know I could miss anyone so much. Hope you are feeling OK. Over the cold, I mean.

Gosh! Have things ever changed back here. We have so many new men on here. Guess I can stand it till I get out. I hear we are going to be here at Terminal Island until Feb. 15th.

The boys all knew I was engaged before I got back. See how news travels?

By the way, honey, I forgot Jo Marie's phone number and I find I don't have their address, so if you want you can send them. I may get into L.A. again, I hope.

Also, darling, let's forget about you coming out Christmas. I know I couldn't get off for five days until after next leave party comes back. Besides, I think we should wait to get married until you have finished high school anyway. What do you think?

Tell Lorenelle I said for her to keep you out of trouble but have a good time.

Well, sweetheart, I warned you my letters would be short, so bye for now, and write.

I love you,
Bert

[I know he is wise telling me not to come to California at this time. However, I miss him and California as well, and I would jump on a train headed west right now if I could.]

December 11, 1945

My Darling,

Nothing to do so I'll scribble you another line to let you know I'm thinking of you all the time. Boy, honey, I'm going nuts out here. I'm so damn lonesome to see you and to think I've only been gone five days. I never knew the "love bug" could bite so hard.

Oh, yeah, when I got back they put me in charge of the Mess Hall instead of doing KP, so I sit and tell the others to work now. I'm really crabby, too.

I went into San Pedro last night to see a movie. It's only a couple of blocks from where we are tied up. I almost got into a fight but my good nature stood between us. It was only a drunk sailor so I overlooked it.

How's school? I hope you are able to concentrate on your lessons in place of me. If you are feeling the way I do I can imagine how much studying you do.

Haven't heard from you yet but I hope to get a letter today. Gosh! I wish you were through school. I'd make (?) you come out here and live until I get out of the Navy. I have every night off until 6 o'clock of a morning. I hear Dick was kind of disappointed because I left and he was still without a brother-in-law.

[Don't tempt me about coming to California. I'm more than willing to do so. School means nothing to me now. I want to be with you.]

Boy, I've sure done some cussing since I came back. We are supposed to get a nine day leave in Feb. I'll be out of the Navy by then, so guess it won't be doing me much good.

Well, Hon, I'm out of wind. Just remember I'm thinking of you and I hate being away from you as bad as you hate for me to be. I love you, Your future Hubby

Dec. 12, 1945
"2 O'clock to be exact."

Darling,

Gosh! Seems swell to hear from you again. I received two swell letters today and almost ate both of them getting at those kisses.

You talk about being sad. What do you think of me? I'm really blue. There are only a couple of guys left on this ship that I know, so I really have a time keeping my mind off you. I'm so damn homesick for you I'm about to die, and speaking of dying there is a woman over here that needs a blood transfusion and it is my type blood so they asked if I'd donate a pint. I guess someone else is going to have some Judkins blood in her. I hope it doesn't make her as mischievous as I.

Oh, yes! Don't forget your love would like a picture sent this way and, sweetheart, spend the money any way you like. If you ever need more, remember I'm as good as your husband so don't be afraid to ask for it. I'm serious.

Sure wish Homer was serious about bringing you out, but don't you ever get the idea you are going to ride a train out or back by yourself. Coming back I saw the way a group of sailors took care of one girl and I'd be worried every day you were on that train. Anyway, I'll be home in Feb. to stay.

Do I ever have a headache. The laundry is broken so I have to wash my clothes by hand. Wish you were here, you could do it for me. I can see that! Ha! Guess I'll have to stay on the ship tonight. Oh, well. I've seen all the movies in Pedro anyway and that's as far as I go. By the way, if you ever need to call me my phone number is Terminal 2-9794.

Well, darling, I've about run out of things to talk about so guess I'll have to bring this to a halt.

Love forever and forever
Elbert "D" for

_____!

PS. Tell Lorenelle I
still love her, too.

Dec. 14,1945

My Sweetheart,

Everyone has gone ashore so I at least have peace and quiet. I need it, the way I feel. I was into L.A. to see if I have the right type of blood for my woman. Well, I do, damn it. Now don't be alarmed, the woman is too old for me and besides she's going to have a baby in Feb. I did see a cute little nurse but none can compare with my own back home.

Never heard from you today. I was expecting it, too. I've written you every day since I've been back. I imagine I have lots more time for writing letters than you. I spend most of the day sleeping around and have been taking in a movie every night. Have to do something to keep my mind off you or I'll die.

[Lorenelle and I have imaginary friends we call Joe and Josephine. When we get into a little trouble, or make unwise decisions, or when things go wrong we say, "Joe, or Josephine did it," or, "They made us do it," or, "It is Joe's fault, not ours." Bert thinks it is funny, and is now doing the same thing. Joe and Josephine are his friends, too. He took Josephine back to California with him.]

I'm sending Josephine back to Joe so he will leave you alone. She is mean to me. She says she is homesick. So am I.

Say, hon, if you see any of the folks, you can tell them you hear from me occasionally because I'll be darned if I intend to write them. Don't have the necessary ambition it takes to write a letter to anyone except you.

[For someone who hates to write letters, you have done a wonderful job writing to me the past few years.]

Have you heard from Bobby? I've been watching the ships come in and they are sure loaded. I was in hopes he could be on one. I'll bet Mary Jo would love to see her Daddy, too. Kids always love their Daddys most because they never whip them, while mothers do. Gosh!

I'll be glad when I can have two little blue-eyed girls of my own. I love kids and I still have my mind made up about little girls.

Bet your dad was glad to see me go, wasn't he? At least he still has his daughter and if I would have stayed longer I'm afraid he wouldn't have had.

Darling, I need a bath dreadfully bad so it's time to say goodnight and pleasant dreams. I'll be thinking of you (as if I could forget you).

Love always
Elbert

P.S. Bet you wish you were here to wash my back. I do too. I love you, honey.

Dec. 15, 1945

To the Sweetest, Swellest,
Bestest person in the world,

That's saying a lot isn't it? I mean it though, darling. I really miss you, hon. Can't seem to get anything done but think of you. I don't mind though, only it is awful to be so darn lonesome. I'd much rather be with you for always. It won't be long until we will be together and for good.

I'm really having a tough time getting this written. More darn interruptions. Oh, well! I've got all afternoon to finish it.

How's school and you agreeing? I'm glad the teachers weren't too hard on you in making up the work you missed. If anyone gets mean to you just let me know.

[My heart isn't in school these days. It is with my good-looking sailor in San Pedro, California. Even the approach of Christmas, a favorite time of year for me, isn't exciting this year. The cold, snowy winter winds howl outside and make me long for the warmth of my sweetheart's arms.]

I imagine Indianola is still as dead as ever. I know one good thing about it. There are some wonderful people there.

What do you know, I never went to shore again last night. Doing pretty good. There isn't anything to do anyway, only go to a movie and I'm getting tired of them.

This letter sure doesn't make sense does it? I seem to just rattle on and on and never say anything. I've hopes of hearing from you today but the mail hasn't come on yet.

Are you rid of your fever sores yet? I hope so, sweet. Mine are gone but I'd love to catch some more from you since I gave you those. It's a wonder Lorenelle doesn't have some. Remember I kissed her goodnight once?

Darling, I'm running short of news. It's getting about supper time and I want to get the boys to work, so guess I'd better close this. I've been doing pretty good lately, a letter every day. Even if they don't say much you know I love you ever so much. I'll be thinking of you, sweet.

Love and Kisses
E.J.
(Future husband)

P.S. Tell Lorenelle I'm sending her my love, too. Well, it's a different kind of love but tell her I said hello.

[It is a good thing Lorenelle is my best friend or I might be jealous.]

P.S. Don't smoke any cigarettes, PERIOD! If you do, well, Brat. (I don't mean that.) I still will get mad when I think of that night.

[Lorenelle and I sneak a cigarette once in awhile. It isn't wise to do that in front of Bert. He hates for women to smoke. He thinks it is alright for men to smoke, however!]

Hell of a paper but best I could do tonight.

Sept.18, 1945
*(Opps, wrong
month, it is
December, 1945)*

My Darling wife (to be),
(Thought it but if
I added that your mom
might see it and think it true.)
This is the third letter I've started to you this eve. Just not in the right spirit. I could swear every other word but don't suppose you care to hear my sob story anyway. Everything has gone wrong since I came back.

I was on the beach Sat. night and two soldiers beat the h--- out of me. They were drunk. As a result I have a cut on the forehead and a rib that's fractured. Guess you know I won't even go to see another movie. These guys are all crazy out here.

Well, sweet, I hope you get your job at the newspaper office.

[I didn't get the newspaper job. I am very disappointed.]

Gosh! I'd love to be back home with you. I just about go nuts out here. I can't tell you how much I miss you and all I do is lay around and think about you. I did have a job here of nights but the captain went over and had us fired. We were making $10.00 a night here in the shipyard and that Son of a b---- had to stop it.

Dearest, I count on being home in Feb. (to stay.) Can't get discharged out here unless your wife is here. Unlucky me doesn't have a wife yet. I will someday though, won't I?

I still can't make up my mind what I want to do when I get out. I'd like to get in a business of my own but $? $? $?

[What about the GI Bill we are hearing of. Sounds like it is government loans for veterans to either go to school, buy a home, or go into business. Perhaps you have not heard of that?]

I received another swell letter from you today. I don't know what I'd do if I didn't hear from you. You have sure been doing wonderful since I came back. Guess you really do love me. I thought you were only kidding. Don't take me seriously.

Doesn't this letter make sense? I can't even think straight anymore. I'm telling you, if anything would happen between me and you I'd go crazy, no kidding. I'm about that way now just being away from you.

How is everyone around home? I hope they are all over their colds. Have you gotten rid of the fever sore? That was mean of me to kiss you when I had mine but gosh! I had to.

Guess you know I missed writing to you a couple of days. I just can't think of anything to say. There is never anything happening around here and you should know that I do love you.

I'm going into L.A. one night next week with a buddy. He wants me to come out home with him to supper. I have hopes you will have sent me Tommy's address and I'll call him. I'd better not go see him. He might decide he didn't want me for a brother-in-law.

Have you seen Clyde Jones around there? If you do and he has anything bad to say about me, don't believe it. My buddy filled him full of a lot of (BS) and he believed it, so I hear but don't you, period.

I'm going to have to speed this up. It's getting late and believe me, I'm sleepy. I've just slept all day today. I'm a boss now, I can do that. The Navy will certainly never get any more work out of me and I think they have given up trying.

If you see Theo's, tell them I think of them even if I don't write. I haven't written to anyone but you since I came back. I wouldn't write to you but I know you would be mad. I love you truthfully but gosh! I hate to write letters. I do love to get them though.

Well, sweetheart, I'd better ring off. It's now midnight so goodnight and sweet dreams. I love you more than anyone in the world.

Your darlin'
B.J.

Dec. 19, 1945

Darling,

At last I succeeded. I've run all over this ship to find some paper to write on. I can never think to buy any when I'm in town. I can't think <u>period</u>!

I received another letter from you today. The fact is I received two but one was dated Sept. 18th.

I'm not making liberty tonight. Just isn't anything to do unless you date and I can't see that. I consider myself married and I'll be darned if I'll step out on you.

Well, hon, if I get into L.A. and can find my way around I intend to go out and see Tommy and the rest. Sure, I'll give Mary Jo a kiss for you but maybe her mother has taught her sailors were bad people.

Indianola sure has a swell basketball team, don't they? Ha! Oh, well, someone has to lose.

Gosh! Hon, if it's so cold back there why don't you pack up and come out here? I'd love to have you. If you can't find a place to stay you can stay on the ship with me. Of course, we would have to get married. I freeze here. Have to use a blanket every night.

There goes that song again "White Christmas." That sure cheers me! The way I feel tonight I'd do anything. Man, do I ever get disgusted. Time goes so slow now that I want to get back home with you.

Am I ever getting fat since I came back and went to bossing in the place of working. All I do is eat and sleep. I got up at 6 this morn, back to bed at 8 and slept till 4 this afternoon. Of course, the boys don't do much work while I sleep but I don't blame them. We have all fresh foods now. I practically live on milk and ice cream.

I thought Homer was leaving to go to school. Speaking of school, I doubt if I get my diploma although I have been highly recommended for it. I only need two credits to get it.

[Yes, he does get his high school diploma from Liberty Center High School when he gets home. He has enough credits from his classes in the Navy to qualify for it.]

Hon, I've got to take a shower, so better ring off. I think of you all the time. Write every day if you aren't too busy. Gosh! If I can't have you out here the least you can do is send me a letter.

Love forever,
Bert

Dec. ?
Wed. 11 O'clock
(Kind of early to
be coming home)

Darling,
Nothing much going on in the city tonight so I came back early as usual. I just had to leave the ship. It's too dull a life to stay aboard.

Kind of had a little excitement for awhile. Me and another sailor went into a bar for a bite to eat when a damn drunk woman came over and sat down. I didn't mind that but she tried to kiss me and that done it. I cussed her a while and the bartender finally called a taxi and sent her out. I don't share my love or kisses with but one person – <u>you</u>! The woman was old enough to be my grandmother.

Never heard from you today. I hope you are OK. It worries me when I don't hear. I'm afraid Juddy has come back. I was only joking but I do look forward for your letters.

Hey, you won't say much if I make this kind of short, will you? I'm sleepy but I promise to write another tomorrow.

Well, hon, I hope to hear from you soon. Until then, All my Love

E.J.

Dec. 20, 1945

My Darling,

In fact the dearest and most wonderful darling in the whole world. It's kind of late for me to be writing but I have to get this in the mail tomorrow.

I was in the city of San Pedro tonight. I'll tell you why though. I got into a little quarrel and broke the crystal out of my watch and took it over for repairs. I've just had the watch a week.

I sure did some cussing. While I was over there I took in a movie. I'm trying to think of the name but can't so you can imagine about how good it was.

I wrote to Lorenelle last night. Of course, I wrote to you first. I sure hate to write. Sometimes if I thought it wouldn't make you mad I'd stop completely.

Tell Lorenelle if she doesn't quit trying to get you to go out she's going to make me awfully mad.

I had a big temptation today. One of the boys brought his wife and her girlfriend here today. He asked me to go out with them. He said she was a swell girl so I studied for a second and then I knew they didn't come any sweller than you. I wouldn't step out on you for the world and I'm not just saying that because I could and you would never know it but if a guy isn't true, well, he's just not in love. I am and it hurts just to be away from you. Boy, if you were out of school you would be right here with me. I really wonder if you feel towards me like I do you. I won't ever need to worry if you do.

Kitty, I'm sleepy as heck so I have to make this short. I had to write this. I don't like for you to be disappointed when you don't find a letter. Goodnight, darling, and remember I'll always love you ever and ever so much.

Your Sweetheart

Dec. 20, 1945
11:15

Sweetheart,

Can't sleep so I'll answer the wonderful letter I received from you again today. Say, you are doing O.K., much better than I expected. I supposed you would forget me when I came back. Keep those letters coming. They help lots in keeping me home. I can hardly control myself among all these temptations but when I think of you it slows me down. I have a darling at home and I know it. I wouldn't give up you for all the wh---s on the west coast.

Well, it's raining in sunny California tonight. I guess it's almost time for the rainy season out here. It really seems cold outside.

Gosh! Do I ever wish you were coming out with your Uncle Glen. I couldn't see you riding the train back by your lonesome though. Of course, I'll be making that trip back in February if you want to wait. I'll have enough points to get out the first of February and that's for certain. I lack 3/4ths of a point or I'd be home in January. I've really been doing some swearing. I don't think they have figured it right. Ha! I have my fingers crossed. Nothing I'd like more than to have you here but please don't come unless you have a way back, <u>please.</u>

Well, sweet, I don't know when the heck I'll be back in L.A. Honest, I hardly leave the ship for more than a couple of hours. There isn't anything to do if you don't drink or go with the women except go to a movie and I'm sure tired of those.

I got a letter from my buddy today. He wants me to come to Chicago and get a job where he is working. He's the one I told you lived in Michigan. He's a swell guy but I imagine the farther I stay away from him the better off I'll be because he's really an ornery cuss and he can usually persuade me to do anything. He doesn't know we are back in the States and we beat him back.

I hear the Army is lowering their points. Maybe Bobby will get home. Gosh! I hope so just for Mary Jo's sake and of course, for the rest.

Gosh! Am I ever getting sleepy. I got up at noon today. I'm not used to getting up so early. One of these days an officer will catch me sleeping in and I'll be shot. Bet you would hate that. Ha- ha!

You know what? I did a good deed today. Butter is ever so hard to get out here. Well, a civilian asked me to get him a pound since I have the keys to the ice box, so I did it. He wanted it for Christmas. Now, was that kind of me? Wow! I sure wouldn't want anyone to see me do that.

I was just thinking, which hand are you wearing the ring on? Don't take me seriously. I know you are true blue to me. There's just one thing, sweet, if you go out never tell me because if you do it will only make me mad and for once I've never cast an eye at another girl.

I see some of the boys are drifting back from the beach. I guess they got their fill early. Liberty just isn't worth a darn here. Too many sailors.

Honey, I've just gotta close. Here's hoping I hear from you tomorrow, Dec. 21. I love you, honey, with every bit of my heart. In fact, I don't believe my heart is with me anymore. I can't even feel it beat.

**Your Beloved
Sailor
E. (D for ?) J**
*[He doesn't like
his middle name,
David, and says
the D stands
for Damn.]*

Dec. 22, 1945

My Darling Kathryn,

Really I don't know what I'm going to write about but I'll try to rattle off something.

Gee! I wish I could be with you this weekend. I've got four days to spend as I please and I'll very likely stay aboard this thing. I don't see why they couldn't have added all these days I'm getting to my leave. They don't need me here anyway. I don't work and, gosh, anyone can be a boss. Even you. I just wonder how henpecked I'll be.

It's still raining tonight in California. Boy, it's been a miserable old day. I didn't even attempt to make liberty tonight. Afraid the grass was wet. Hope it's still raining in the morn. We have a Captain's Inspection tomorrow before we can leave. Boy, I hate these brass hats. They are usually giving me h--- for something or other. They have been kind of good lately but it's a trick. They want us to sign over.

What kind of mischievousness have you and Lorenelle been in lately? Just so you leave the boys alone.

Did Richard and Homer go to Missouri? I've never heard from any of the folks but you. That's all that matters anyway. If I don't hear from them I won't write.

You know what I was just counting? The letters you have written me since I came back. The number is 32. Didn't suppose you would do that good. I wouldn't want you to neglect your schoolwork for me, so just write when you aren't too busy.

I can't think of a darn thing more to say so just as well quit. I do love you, honey, ever and ever so much. I'll be home to stay in February.

Forever Yours
Elbert

December 24, 1945

My Darling Sweetheart,

As usual I'm having difficulty in thinking of something to write you.

I've been kind of blue until today and I received two letters from you. I feel O.K. now. Odd what a little letter can do for you.

Guess my worries are over if your Uncle Glen came out without you. I wanted you to come so bad but gosh! I couldn't see my hon riding that train back by herself.

You must have been in an awful mood when you wrote this letter. Indianola isn't so bad, California stinks too. Will I ever be glad to get off this coast. All I've seen since I came back is a bunch of damn drunks, women included. Guess that's why I never go ashore.

Speaking of me calling you, send me your phone number and I promise the next opportunity I get I will call.

I was going out to Jo Marie's Saturday, but jeepers I hate to go out there. Bashful!

Did you have a Merry Christmas? Since I'm writing this the 24th, I can't tell you whether I did or not.

Darling, I'm going to close this for now. I'll finish it tomorrow. It wouldn't get sent off in the mail before Wednesday anyway.

8 o'clock Dec. 25

I swear I'll get this in the mail sooner or later. I can just see you waiting in the post office four days straight without getting a letter. I really don't know why I haven't written. My intentions have always been good, but ... ???

I do think of you constantly. All day today you were on my mind.

And I do hope you did have a very Merry Christmas.

I wasn't so merry today but oh! last night. We really threw a party. It was aboard ship but I did have some fun. I ended up by drinking one too many Coke highs. Everyone who was asleep at midnight I woke him up and told him it was Christmas. Some got rather mad but I didn't care. That's the first time I've raised heck since I came back. I'm sorry of it now. Got to have some fun once in awhile after all. I do leave the women alone. You ought to be thankful for that. I'm true but only because you are too. It's a good thing I put a ring on your finger.

I love you, honey, but I have to close this thing. I've run out of things to rattle about. Here's hoping I get a letter from you tomorrow. Until then, I'll be thinking, dreaming and wishing to heck I were home with you. I'll love you always.

Love and a great
big kiss,
Elbert

Christmas 1945

This is the first Christmas in many years the world is at peace. We all rejoice because many of our military loved ones are home since the war first began. Many are still in faraway places keeping the peace and restoring order in the devastated regions that were in the midst of the turmoil. There is terrible sadness for the families of the ones who will never come home.

December in our small Midwestern town is a festive time. Fresh cut evergreen trees are adorned with handmade decorations and berry and popcorn garlands.

Everyone attends church and give thanks for the end of the worldwide war. Our majestic old stone Methodist Church in Indianola, Iowa, is covered with garlands of evergreen, candles and holly berries. The fragrance lingers in the air.

The town square wears evergreen as well. An occasional string of large brightly colored Christmas lights can be seen here and there.

Some store windows proudly display the few Christmas treasures that can be obtained during this post war season. Icy air makes our fingers and toes tingle from the cold. Faces are bright red while people stand around the streetlights as flakes of snow fall softly on our muffled shoulders. This is the first time in years we are allowed to turn all of these lights on. The fear of an attack from foreign airplanes is gone.

Carolers walk about and gaily sing Christmas songs, sleigh bells ring and almost everyone is happy at this peaceful time.

But I'm not. For the first time in my life I'm not excited about the holidays. I've lost interest in high school, basketball games and going out with friends. I miss Elbert D., who is still aboard ship in San Pedro Harbor in California. He seldom mentions Christmas in his letters because he is so homesick and lonely. I should have gone to California on the train with Uncle Glen when I had the chance. Bert and I could be married by now. My brother Tom lives there, as do other family members I could live with. I am tired of winter in Iowa, school and waiting for my sweetheart to come home.

Dec. 26, 1945
Wed. eve, 8 O'clock

Hi Honey,

I don't know what the heck keeps me on here but here I am, writing letters instead of on liberty. Writing to you is the best way to spend my liberties anyway. I can keep out of trouble, anyway.

Got a letter from you today and also a Christmas card from both you and Lorenelle. I didn't send out any cards so guess I'd better write Lorenelle or she might get kind of sore. Of course I'm not worried about you.

Gosh, darling, what kind of guy do you think I am? I don't care if you go car riding with boys <u>ONLY</u> Richard's age. Let people talk as long as I don't care. Why should they?

[Richard and his friends are two years younger than Lorenelle and I.]

Well, today ends another day of my Navy life. Only 37 more of those horrible days and I'll be coming back to you to stay. Believe me, I can hardly wait. I long for you more every day. I almost go crazy around here. Not many boys left here that I know. I don't dare go out with these because I know what they are going out for. This stuff isn't for me.

Suppose you are still freezing back there. Gee! Wish I were there to help keep you warm. It's nice and warm here but I hate California. I'LL LIVE ANYWHERE BUT HERE. The civilians can't even get butter out here.

[We can't get butter, or many other commodities that had been rationed in Iowa, either.]

Everyday someone comes to me and says, "Hey! How about a pound of butter?" Somehow they know I have keys to it. I could get rich off them, but not me. I don't care to hang by a rope since I have you.

The Captain has darn near given me the works once since I came back and I don't care to go before him again. All the officers aboard here know me by my first name now. I won't tell you why.

[Could it be because you and some of the boys threw buckets of paint over the side instead of painting the ship like you were ordered to?]

How's your mom and the rest? I sure think they are all swell.

I even hate to take their daughter away from them but I'm going to.

Boy! I can hardly wait to get your picture. You shouldn't keep me in suspense. I've never seen you in a bathing suit. Are you sending any of those to me?

Boy, the noise in here is terrible. I can't think, let alone write. The radio is on to the fullest extent.

When's vacation ended? Bet even the way you hate school you will be glad to get back. You don't really hate it, do you?

[No.]

Does Lorenelle still hear from Loren?

My darling, I'm very sleepy and you know what that means. I do love you ever so much but just can't think of any more to say.

Love always, Bert

P.S. Can't show you how much I love you in a letter. But just wait until I come home.

So, you are sending Joe out here to keep me out of trouble. He isn't here yet. He probably got in trouble on the way here.

Dec. 27, 1945
7 o'clock

My Honey,

Another day of awfully hard work has ended and I'm almost too tired to write letters but I've got to answer the two swell letters I received from you today. If Joe would hurry and get here I'd make him serve my meals in bed and I wouldn't have to get up. Boy, I'm lazy since I came back. I weigh 155 pounds now but am afraid I'm going to lose it all.

[He only weighed 126 pounds when he came home on leave in November! The war in the Pacific did that to him.]

Remember,

I told you I had a drink Christmas eve? Well, I'm not over the effects of it yet. All I can keep down is milk. I swear, never again. That all happened right aboard ship, too. I can still keep my head up because I'm not like most sailors here.

These married men are worse than I. One thing I don't do is step out on you and believe me, I won't. I love you too much for that. Every time anyone asks me to go on liberty with them I think of some excuse and usually end up writing to you. I've been ashore three times since I came back.

Gosh! You must be having lots of snow back there now. Guess you really had a white Christmas. I hope your Dad didn't have to work that day.

[Dad works for the State Highway Commission, along with Bert's brother, Theo, and they have to clear the roads when it snows.]

Gee! I'm so darn blue tonight. I can hardly write. I want to get home so bad. I wouldn't know why! Guess I can stand it if you can.

Wish to heck I knew what I was going to do when I get out of here. I did know what I was going to do but since we have made up my plans have changed considerably. I'll find a way to take care of a wife or else there won't be a wife, even if I do love you.

Back to writing. I stopped to drink some milk and talk over the cups. I was telling one of the guys all about you. You should have been a little mouse and heard me. Of course, it was all good. I don't think he believed me. Most of the guys don't. They just say sucker and laugh. My temper is worse than ever now. I had the nerve to tell off a Naval officer today. The first time in my whole life. I don't know what made me do it but I got away with it. I've got to control that temper, too, for things like that they could make me stay in the Navy for six months and that would kill me.

Jeepers, I can hardly wait for your pictures to get here. Maybe I'll get them tomorrow. I hope so.

Darling, it looks like the end again, so I'll sign off by saying goodnight and I love you with all my heart.

As good as your
husband
Bert

Sun eve.
Dec. 31, 1945

My Darling Sweetheart,

Sunday night and here I am aboard. Boy! Am I getting tired of this kind of life. And to think I've got this weekend off and Monday and Tuesday. Oh, well! I can stand it for another 30 days. Thank the Lord that's all I have left and then I can come home and be with you.

I received another letter from you Saturday. I couldn't answer it then because mail doesn't go out on Sundays and I didn't feel like putting on blues and going into Pedro to mail it. I'll make up for it tonight anyway.

Gee, I hope this next year brings forth a lot of happiness for you and me. If I'm with you I know I'll be happy. I sure hope we can get married. I'm sure planning on it. The boys all say I act more like a married man now than most of these married men but why shouldn't I? I've found the girl I want. She's wonderful, too.

Your vacation will soon be over, won't it? Oh, well! This is your last semester and then you will wish you were back in school! After all you can have a lot of fun going to school. I take it that it was snowing back there Christmas. You said your dad had to work. I hope it stops that before I come back or I'll probably freeze.

That Tabu Joe put on your letter sure smells good. You had better be careful who you wear that around. All those Indianola brats will be after you. I'm worried too, like heck. By the way, I thought Joe was on his way to California!

How is Lorenelle? I think she is pretty swell. I'm happy you two are friends.

I've been up listening to records all afternoon. I didn't get up until noon. Boy, if I'd ever get caught in bed that late I hate to think what would happen. I just don't care anymore.

Darling, I'm out of wind! You know I do love you and that's all that matters.

I'll always love you
BJ

[Happy New Year. Welcome 1946.]

Chapter 25

My Dear, Dearest, Sweetheart, (Sounds like I might have more than one, but really, truly, I haven't),

Everything is peaceful around here so I'll start the New Year right by writing you a note.

Some night I had last night. I spent New Year's on this thing. I had an invitation to a party, too. I knew what would take place if I went so I decided just to stay cooped up. Never even had a drink. Pretty good if I do say so myself. That's a New Year's resolution.

Gee, darling, your pictures came yesterday. Boy, they were perfect. I showed them to everyone aboard ship. I do believe the colored one was the best. You looked too ornery in the other but I love them both. I also got a letter from you. You have ruined me because I look for one of those every day and am usually disappointed if I don't hear from you.

It's a good thing you don't smoke. I love you lots more, honey, so please keep right on leaving them alone. Boy, was I ever mad that night you lit that one. I was almost sorry I had made up with you.

You are all I have ever dreamed of if you will just leave cigarettes alone. Guess I'll never be able to understand women but I can't understand why they want to be tough. If I had to pick that kind of girl I'd never get married. I make a good preacher, don't I? Honey, I love you and I just don't want anything to come between us.

I know you are wonderful and I don't want anything to come between us.

Well, am I uncle yet? Oh, yes, I gave Winnie orders that if she had a baby boy she wasn't to call it Elbert. You are all that ever writes me so all the news I get is what you write.

Did you get your job? I hope you did. It will make the rest of the school year go faster.

Gee, I'm glad Bobby has headed back. [My brother Bob was a foot soldier on Okinawa.]

Sure hope I'm home when he gets back there. Gosh, I have to see my brother-in-law but, jeepers, I just can't make myself go into L.A. to see them. [After all of this time away from home, he is still the shy Iowa farm boy.]

What a letter. I go rattling on and don't even remember what I say. Oh, well, since it's to you, I'm sure you won't mind. I do love you and, after all, a letter is just to let each other know that we are thinking of one another.

It shouldn't take a letter for that because that's all I do is think of you. I can't stand it out here without you. I've wished a million times we had gotten married and you were here with me.

That Jones boy from Indianola got back off leave. He said it was really cold back there. Glad I took my leave in November.

Honey, I love you ever so much but I have to close. No more to write about. You will probably think I've gone crazy when you read what I have written.

All my love,
Elbert

P.S. I am sure anxious for this month to pass so I can get home with you. I miss you, honey. Here's hoping I get a letter tomorrow; haven't gotten any for a day. A whole day, can you imagine that? I'll be dreaming about you. Tell Joe that Josephine is finally on her way home. Where is he anyway, coming here, or is he there?

Good night
darling

Jan. 5, 1946

Sweetheart,

I should start this out very mushy because by the time you get this you are really going to be sore at me. I'm on my knees. Please forgive me for not writing but I didn't hear from you for four whole days and then I got four letters at once. The mail got fouled up somehow. Again – I'm sorry and I won't let it happen again. I thought you were mad at me.

Well my racket has finally ended. I am no longer a boss or I'm not doing K.P. I've been off one day and what happens, the Captain holds an inspection and now I'm confined to the ship for 10 days. My dress blues had Seaman Second Class on them and they should have had S 1/C. That doesn't worry me. When it gets dark I'll get off this thing. We are tied up to a dock and it's only a short jump from the ship to the dock. No fooling, the kind of mood I've been in I don't give a hoot if they keep me in this outfit for 6 years. Yes I do but only because you are back there. If it wasn't for you I'd be raising he-- out here but every time I start to do anything I think of how bad I want to get back there with you. No fooling, if I tried I couldn't love anybody else but you.

I saw a good movie last night "Leave Her to Heaven." If you get the chance you ought to see it. It's about a jealous woman. Now don't take that expression wrong. I know you aren't jealous. Well, anyway, not much. Maybe you aren't any more. [Editor's note: "Leave Her to Heaven" was a 1945 film directed by John M. Stahl. It starred Gene Tierney, who received a best actress Academy Award nomination for her role, Cornel Wilde and Jeanne Crain. It was 20th Century Fox's most successful film of the 1940s.]

Boy, you must have been in a good mood Saturday night. A kiss on every page. I'd like them much better if they were real.

Guess I don't have any excuse for not calling you now since I have your telephone number except it's impossible for 10 days starting today.

I'm sure counting the days when I can get home with you. I want to be there when you break your neck and, honey, if you don't stay out of those cars that's what is going to happen! No, I'm not trying to be bossy but I would rather have you in one piece. There isn't any use of me telling you anything while I'm 2000 miles from you, is there?

You can tell Neil he has my permission to take you out, as if he needed it. He is your first cousin, and my best friend. Hey, who are you trying to fool? I know if you wanted to go out you wouldn't ask me and I doubt if you would tell me. Honey, I'm hard to get along with these days. When I'm with you again I'll never be mean to you.

Guess you are the first girl that ever had me wrapped around her little finger, and me a sailor! Oh, well! All sailors can't be bad anyway but I've got to see the first one on this ship that isn't. They all belong to the 4F Club. If you don't know what that stands for I'll tell you when we get married.

Has Bobby gotten back in the States yet? Jeepers, I sure hope so. Is he getting discharged when he gets back or do you know?

I'm getting in a better mood now. Maybe I should tear this up and begin again.

One of the boys was back and asked me if I wanted to go over the fantail on liberty. I said no, like a good boy. I should have said yes because most of the boys have slipped off anyway. Can't afford to take chances. I'm getting out of the Navy the 2nd of February. The Captain loves me anyway. Would love to hang me.

Santa Ana isn't very far from here. Maybe when I get off restriction I can go over there and see your cousin Marilyn.

I sent home my photograph album. If Iris lets you see those pictures don't be angry. Yours are the only ones that mean anything. Rattle, rattle, rattle and I still haven't said anything but I can't end here. There isn't enough room. *[It's the bottom of his page, no place to sign off.]*

Suppose you are back in school again. I hope you had a wonderful vacation but I imagine the weather was kind of miserable. It is out here. I hate this place. You seldom see the sun until noon. I've really got a bad cold in the head, too, although I don't have a pretty little red nose like yours was.

Darling, my gem of the ocean, sweetheart, and all other nice things, I've got to close, take a shower and go to bed. Wish you were here, I'd let you tuck the covers around me. Be good, sweetheart. I'll be thinking of you.

Your love,
Bert

Tell Joe I said he'd better be good. Why did he trip you on the ice while skating? What else does he do beside trip you?

Sunday Jan. 6, 1946

Hi Darling,

This is going to be short and sweet. I can't think of a thing to write, but I'll try.

I do love you, honey, lots and lots and then lots more but when it comes to writing a letter every day there just isn't anything to write about.

Well, sweet, I've got to close. Please believe me, I love you. I'll even send you a big kiss with this letter.

Love
Elbert

Jan. 8, 1946
Tues. 9:15

Dearest Kitty,

Sweetheart, I'll try and write a letter tonight in place of a note. That was a note I wrote yesterday and a short one at that. I told you I still loved you and that's all that matters.

I love you as much as your parents do or I wouldn't want to take you away from them. I may be ornery but I'd never do anything to hurt you.

Gosh! I know Jo Marie wants me to come over but I just can't. You know I've never met her and I am so shy.

Boy! I did the craziest thing last night and, well, the night before too. I jumped ship just to go see a movie. I went right up town in overalls too. If I had got caught! Tonight I'm staying aboard ship,

I've only got 8 days restriction left. It's hard for me to be good. The other night, someone came in and turned on the lights and I got up and broke all of the light bulbs. I was mad. They were all drunk and raising heck. This is the craziest bunch of sailors I ever saw. I should be in bed sleeping now because they will be coming back from liberty soon. Oh! I'll be glad when I can come home with you. You are about the only person who could ever make me behave. Guess I would never be the same kind of guy if it weren't for you.

Boy! Is it ever cold out here. I freeze every night and I sleep with all my clothes on and two blankets. Guess I'm just a sissy. What will I do when I come home?

There isn't anything more to tell you, only I do think of you all the time and I love you more and more and more every day.

Love
Bert

Jan. 10, 1946

My darling Kathryn,

Gee, honey, every time I say I love you I think of what a crazy person I was to think that you didn't care for me before I got home. I didn't even want to see you when I came home. And now look! I'm going nuts if I don't get home soon.

I almost started a free-for-all last night. I just can't keep my mouth shut until someone tries to shut it for me. I go around with a chip on my shoulder all the time.

I'm counting the days until I get out of here – 23 more left and I'll be heading home. I think that's the reason I am so hard to get along with. I sure hope they don't keep Bobby overseas but those in control will do anything. Maybe he will get to come anyway. Jeepers, I haven't been to L.A. for ages so haven't seen Jo Marie. Maybe if I can get some courage I'll go over before I have to leave. But no promises.

Well, I hear we have some hot water, so must hurry and get a bath.

I've really been working hard trying to stay away from the bosses. They won't even let me sleep anymore. If they want any work done bad they usually do it themselves because I play for an hour before doing it.

Please don't quarrel with your mom. She is awfully good to you. How many mothers let their 15-year-old daughter go out with someone my age when they are that young? Remember? Are you going to let our two little daughters go out when they are that young? Now don't say we aren't going to have girls 'cause we are! Ha!

They held a roll call at 8 tonight and don't think I wasn't glad to be here. Six guys were missing and I hate to think what they will get. Better close now, I love you with all my heart.

Love,
Bert

I haven't heard my heart beat since I was home, you must have it.

Jan. 12, 1946

My Darling,

I got two letters from you today. Guess you know it made me feel awfully good. I didn't get any yesterday and was disappointed. I know I shouldn't expect one every day when I don't write every day.

There isn't a day goes by but what I think of you. Wish you were here. I'm going to try and slip off and go to the horse races tomorrow. The Captain won't be back till Monday and he is the only one that worries me. We could really have some fun. There is really lots happening in California, but I don't like it. Guess it is like you say, I only see the bad part but what I see I hate. I love lots of excitement but not the kind where a bunch of drunks are spoiling the fun.

I haven't heard from the girls lately. Hazel wrote me once and all she talked about is you. No fooling, I believe my sisters would shoot me if we broke up. They love you almost as much as I do, ALMOST!! I'll never disappoint them, I swear. I'm ready to get married now on love alone. That's really what counts anyway.

Say, remember that boo-hoo card you and Joe sent me? Well, I just got it today. Guess poor Joe really did hate for me to leave. Well Joe, twenty-one more days and I'll be heading home and we can both push Kathryn down on the ice!

Gee! Honey, I really am lonesome for you tonight. I think the longer I am away the more I love you. You are perfect, sweetheart. I always did want you but now my dream is really coming true.

I sure had a time last night. I jumped ship at about 10 O'clock to go get something to eat. One of the boys was coming back from liberty and he saw me. He had his car so he took me into town. Well, we got stopped for speeding. He got turned over to the M.P. and since I wasn't driving I got turned loose. I thought sure as heck they were going to escort me to the ship and that would have been the end. I still shake when I think of it. I should be good but I can't.

I've been working today. I had to, the boss stayed by my side and I couldn't leave. Boy, I hate to work in this outfit and most of the guys know it. The war is over now and I want to go home.

I can barely fit into my blues. I swear, I have to wear them tomorrow. I don't want to buy new ones when I only have a short time before becoming a civilian. Think I'll go on a diet until I get home.

Until tomorrow, I'll close. I love you, darling, very, very much, as if you didn't know. Tell Joe to be good or else! Boys shouldn't trip girls on the ice.

All my love,
Elbert "D"

Jan 14, 1946

Hi Sweet,

I went to Santa Ana to see Marilyn [Hess, later McKee – Ed.] and her folks Saturday. I sure had a swell time. Marilyn called me Saturday morning and wanted to know if I could come out. She really has changed. She's a little lady now. I kind of imagine she is a bit mischievous, but who isn't when they are young? Betty and her husband ["Hoot" Judkins, a distant cousin of Elbert – Ed.] were there. They sure have a sweet little girl. She had more to do with me than my nieces. Your aunt and uncle wanted me to stay all night but, jeepers, I didn't want to stay away too long because I slipped off right after the captain left. Tomorrow my restriction is up and I can leave the ship legally. It won't be any fun to go on liberty then, so guess I'll just sit around and twiddle my thumbs.

In eighteen days I'll be leaving this so and so thing. I don't honestly know whether I'm glad or not. I know I want you and that's really the only reason I'm coming out.

Too much noise here, I can't think.

Gee! I'm glad to hear Tommy and Bobby are going back home. Sure hope they will be there when I get back. I only hope they don't talk you into moving to California. Regardless, hon, I couldn't ever live here. I just don't like it.

I broke my watch again. I will fix it one more time, then if it happens again I will have Josephine throw it over the side. *[I thought Josephine was in Iowa.]*

Boy, she is terrible. Almost getting as bad as Joe. Someone threw all the paint over the side and I'm almost certain it was her. I won't have to do any painting for a while, anyway.

Well, darling, enough said. I love you, dearest, and I'm really keeping track of the days until I can get home with you.

I'll love you forever
E.J.

P.S. You ought to be ashamed beating up poor Joe. Gosh, hon, Indianola is kind of dead and he has to liven it up once in a while.

I love you, sweetheart, more than
I can say in a letter.

Jan 18, 1946

My Darling,
Well, sweetheart, it's been three days since I've written you so maybe I can think of something to write for a change. I doubt it. I can't think, period. Just too much noise.

I looked for a letter from you today but didn't get one. It doesn't make me mad when I don't hear from you like it used to. I know you love me and that's what counts. Just so I get two a week.

Sweetheart, I already have my application in for a job to commence the first of March. I should be getting an answer in a day or so. The location is in El Paso, Texas. *[El Paso, Texas. He will be as far away from me as he is now.]*

I get more disgusted every day at the Navy. I have to work now and I'm not kidding. The captain put out an order that anyone not working will be sent to sea immediately. I wish you could see him. There isn't a person on the ship that likes him. Tonight at 5 minutes till 4 he went into the showers and every guy in there was to stay aboard and work tonight. I'm certainly glad that I only have 16 days left. I'm really being a good little sailor, too. I've got to get out of here.

Do you ever hear anything from the family? I never hear from anyone but you.

I've been wondering how Joe is doing lately. Expect it is too cold for him to be outside much.

Gosh! Honey, wish I were back there with you. I love you so darn much. I'm about the luckiest guy in the world to have a girl as wonderful as you. I really miss you.

I took some pictures the other day. I sure hope they are good. I don't have any pictures of the guys out here.

My blond-headed buddy got back off leave. He's here beside me and is certainly making enough noise. Sometimes I'm inclined to believe he's crazy.

Darling, this isn't much but I've got to get some sleep. Tell Lorenelle hello for me.   Love forever,

                                                                Elbert
                                                        Jan. 19, 1946

Sweetheart,

Only two sheets of paper left so this will be short.

You sound like you are really having problems in school. Grange sounds as if he might be working you kids as hard as our captain. If I wasn't getting out of here soon I'm afraid I'd tell him to kiss my behind. He keeps telling us if we don't work he is going to send us back to sea and I mean that scares me because he could do it. I work, I want to get back with you.

Tomorrow I have a 48-hour liberty. It's Sunday and I can sleep in. I'm staying aboard but I'll leave Monday just to get out of work. Since I'm off restriction I've been staying aboard almost every night.

Things are sure dead around here anymore. Gosh! We used to have some fun once in awhile. Most of the boys are girl crazy now and since I have nothing to do with these girls I'm kind of left out. Some of the beasts they go with, wow!

Did Neil ever come up and take you to a movie? I thought he was getting married. We'll make him take both of us out when I get back. He used to be a swell guy, no kidding. Of course, Army life doesn't help a person but I imagine he is still OK.

One of the boys just saw this letter you wrote me where you said your wife. He thinks I am married now, no fooling. I don't care because I will be before too long. I love you, honey, and I'm certainly not going to let you get away from me now. I almost gave you up once. What a crazy guy I was.

I sure hope it quits snowing when I get home. I hate to sit at home over the register but I guess if it's cold I will have to.

Sweetheart, there is an interruption so I'll close this now. Will write again soon.

I love you lots, honey,
Always, Elbert

Jan. 24, 1946

Dearest Kitty,

Gosh! It's been so long since I've written a letter. I'm sorry, honey, that I haven't written. I don't even have an excuse.

Really, I thought I'd be headed home by now but for some reason they are holding us, the dirty SOBs! I don't know when I'll get there now. Guess you know that really makes me blue because I want to be with you so bad.

Hey, I got my job in Texas if I want it. I really have my doubts if I take it. I want a job where I can take you with me. I'll probably hang around Indianola till you have finished school. Boy, when I get there this time I'll be darned if I ever leave you. I love you, sweetheart.

I'd get married the day I came home if I only knew what I was going to do. I can look out for myself but I don't want you standing on a street corner begging for a dime. I'm afraid I'm not capable of supporting a wife without a good job.

That's sure heck about Bobby. I felt sure he would be home by now but that's the way with this kind of life. They promise you the world but when the time comes they take it away from you.

I received two swell letters from you yesterday. They were the first for several days. I do love to hear from you but when I don't, it doesn't make me mad! <u>VERY!</u>

I hope everyone is feeling O.K. back there. I'll bet it is cold. I could stand it if they would just let me come home. You would help to keep me warm, wouldn't you? I didn't know I could miss anyone so much. Well, I know now. Sure hope I hear from you tomorrow. It does help.

Am I ever sleepy. My sleep was interrupted last night. My buddy came back from liberty and woke me up to tell me he had been robbed. I thought he was just kidding or drunk but he wasn't. Two guys held up the place he was in and took all the money from all the customers. Don't think I haven't been laughing at him. Both guys were killed later. That's what I don't like about California. It isn't safe for a sailor to travel by himself around here and that's no lie. We never leave the ship unless we are in pairs. Oh well! I could say a lot about California but will save my arguments until I get home.

Can't understand why Homer went to Illinois to live but guess he knows. I really don't know what I want to do. I don't have a mind of my own, I guess. I never thought much of civilian life until I'm really getting out and now it scares me. We'll make out, though, won't we? I know I can if I have you to live for. You are wonderful, honey. If ever I were in doubt before I'm certain now.

Isn't this a silly letter? I just ramble from one thing to another. Can't help it. There just isn't anything to write about. Everything remains the same here.

We rise at 6:30, me at 8. That is, we are supposed to get up at 6:30. I usually wait until the captain comes aboard. I quit work at

11:30, eat at 12:00, go back to work at 1:00, quit at 4:00, liberty starts at 4:30. Same thing every day. Isn't that some life? Bah!

I've got to hurry this. I'm really tired. It seems the more I sleep the more I want. I haven't been anywhere for at least a week.

I love you darling. Here's hoping I hear from you tomorrow.

Love forever and ever
Elbert "D."??

P.S. Again, I love you ever so much, honey. Wish I were home with you tonight. It can't be too far away now.

Jan. 28, 1946

Dearest Darling,

Well, sweet, it's really true. I'm writing another letter. Josephine is standing over me with a club. If it wasn't for her I guess you'd never hear from me. Guess you have heard that before.

[Bert hates writing letters, but he has written me at least 200 in the past three years. I think that is above and beyond the call of duty. They are wonderful letters. Charming in fact. I shall treasure them always.]

Honey, I think I am being sent to the separation center for my discharge the first of February. Nothing is certain. I should be gone now but here I still am. Anyway, I'll be home as soon as they will let me come and just to be with you. I could stay here but I don't want to. I hate California.

Gosh! It's been awhile since I've heard from you. When you get this letter you don't have to write me anymore because the letters would probably find me at home.

Jeepers, I hope it warms up back there before I get home or I'll freeze. Sissy, aren't I?

I will be glad to get home. I wonder why? It could be I have the most wonderful girl in the world back there. I love you, honey. Can't stand it to be away from you. No fooling, last night I couldn't sleep because all I could think about was you. I just rolled from one side to the other side of the bed. I was really lonesome for you.

There isn't anything new around here. As many fights and quarrels as ever. Boy, there's a bunch of crazy guys here. Last night, some drunken cuss came in and like to have broken my arm trying to get me out of bed. I was too sleepy to see who it was or I'd probably gotten up. Every night someone comes back to the ship all beaten up.

I don't make a good sailor when I have a sweetheart at home.

How's all the folks at home? Did you get over your sore throat? Did you get down to 115 pounds yet? I know I've sure lost some weight lately. Don't know why. Maybe it is because I can't eat. Just no appetite.

I can't think of any more to say, so goodnight, honey, and I love you with every inch of my heart.

I'll love you forever,
Bert

[Last letter before his discharge from the Navy, February 18, 1946.]

Feb. 11, 1946

My Darling Kitty,

I thought I had better drop you a few lines, it doesn't look like I'll ever get out of this outfit.

I'm in the Receiving Barracks now, waiting on transportation to Minneapolis, Minnisota, for my discharge. I've been here for four days. I have hopes I'll leave by Monday and better still be home by at least the 20th.

I could have written sooner but just didn't. I love you, though, honey, and I do think of you even in my dreams. I hope you aren't mad at me. You aren't, are you?

How's school? Schoolwork better not occupy all of your nights. I've got to have at least two or three a week.

[School is the last thing on my mind these days. I can't think of anything except my sweetheart will soon be home. I'll be lucky if I earn enough credits to graduate with my class. And I don't care!]

I just had a quarrel here. What a quarrel. I have a worse temper than I used to have. I've sure changed a lot since before the war began.

Well, darling, I'm going to close this and here's hoping I see you real soon. I love you ever so much.

Yours forever
Bert

Feb. 20, 1946

As I walk slowly down East Salem Street toward home the giant elm trees on both sides of the street touch each other overhead and make a sparkling ice tunnel that pops and crackles. A winter sun shines down from a cold blue sky. East Salem is a glorious sight on a day like this. Snow banks are piled on both sides of the neatly shoveled walkway. Tidy Midwestern bungalows and some tall Victorian homes line the way. As I approach my white home at 808 East Salem I see someone sitting on the porch steps. I walk closer and a man in a navy blue pea coat stands, and spreads his arms to embrace me. My mother is peeking through the lace curtains in the large front room window. She doesn't want to come outside and interfere in the homecoming of my sailor. I get a short glimpse of her standing there with a white hankie held in her hand beneath her eyes. She closes the curtains and I rush into his arms. I am crying as well, crying with joy. He is really home after three long years. The long wait is done.

Epilogue

Happy Birthday, Darling,

I love you, sweetheart. What do you give your wife on her birthday?

After walking downtown, looking through a few shops, I have no idea what you would want so I decided to buy some writing paper and tell you how much I love you.

I know I don't tell you this very often but you know me, I never could express myself with words, but the feeling has always been there.

Kitty, you have to be the most wonderful person in the world to have lived with me all these 44 years. I know life has sometimes been tough. The good times have outweighed the bad many times. If I could turn back the clock very few things would be changed. I've enjoyed every minute with you. I love you.

My thinker has run out of think so I will close this by saying tell me when and we will go out for dinner.

I love you, love you and love you more.
B.J.

March 30, 2008

On March 30, 2008, family and friends gather on the hilltop outside Orland, California, to say goodbye to our beloved Elbert D. Judkins. We are blessed with a glorious early spring day. The big western sky is filled with flying birds and lazy white clouds. Mt. Lassen and Mt. Shasta stand majestically in the distance. Down below us are lush green fields covered with clusters of golden California poppies and purple lupine. Herds of lowing cattle graze among the flowers. Black chunks of lava rock stand out of the green hills to the west and south. Two deer stand watching on a nearby hill. Tall Black Butte towers over the nearby lake where Bert and I and sometimes a grandchild or two loved to hike and camp and fish. The coastal mountain range hovers between us and the Pacific Ocean. All of our children and grandchildren are here. Our son Richard is leading the memorial service, and our daughter Kathy and our grandson Bill read special stories as two friends softly play on their guitars "The Red River Valley" and other country and western songs Bert loved. Our son Larry and Bert's small terrier Peaches stand by me.

And I am thinking of June 2, 1946, the day Bert and I were married in the Methodist Church in Indianola, Iowa. It was three months after Bert had been discharged from his three years of service in the Navy. Just two weeks before I had graduated from high school. It was a lovely early summer day, much like this one.

Mother and Dad were there. My brother Bob and his wife, Jo Marie, stood with us. Their small daughter Mary Jo sat on her grandmother's lap. Bob had just recently been discharged from the Army after serving in the Battle of Okinawa in the Pacific. My best friend Lorenelle and Bert's friend Neil stood close by, watching the small ceremony. I could see my young brother Richard in the street behind our car, tying tin cans to the back bumper.

And so we began our married life. Bert was studying auto mechanics and the retail business in the local Western Auto store, courtesy of the G.I. Bill. I was happy to be a young housewife and eager to be a mother. Two years later we began our family when Bert's blue-eyed baby girl Kathy arrived. She was soon followed by her two brothers, Richard and Larry. We lived our first fifteen years together in Indianola. Then Bert grew tired of the severe Iowa winter weather so we decided to move to sunny California, where some of our family lived. My widowed father made the move with us. After spending two years there during the war, I had always wanted to return to California. While Bert had hated California when he was in the Navy, he grew to love it after we moved to Santa Fe Springs. He became a successful businessman, owning and operating three Shell Auto Care Centers. I studied nursing and began working in the medical field, continuing that work for the next forty-four years. Upon Bert's retirement, we moved to Orland in rural Northern California, where we have lived happily for twenty-seven years, blessed by our children who gave of themselves to us but also gave us son-in-law Dan and grandson-in-law John, and six grandchildren – Bill, Aileonna, David, Phillip, Robert, and Russell – as well as five great grandchildren – Alexandria, Connor, Calissa, and Michael and Byron.

As I stand in the old country cemetery this March day, 2008, I remember so much, but most of all I remember two young lovers of almost sixty-five years earlier and their long journey.

We have done well together, you and me. Rest easy, my love.

Kitty

[The Destroyer *USS Stevens DD 479* was decommissioned on July 2, 1946, and remained with the Pacific Reserve Fleet in San Diego, California, until December 1, 1972, when her name was struck from the Navy list. On November 27, 1973, her hull was sold to Zidel Explorations, Inc., of Portland, Oregon.

The *Stevens* was awarded nine battle stars for service in World War II.

Elbert D. Judkins S1/C was awarded:

American Area Campaign Ribbon

Asiatic-Pacific Area Campaign Ribbon with 6 bronze stars

Philippine Liberation Ribbon with 2 bronze stars.]